Child Speak Out!

By J. Bridgers

All Rights Reserved. No part of this book should be reproduced or transmitted by means of: electronic and mechanical, this includes: photocopying, recording or any information storage and retrieval system without the permission from the copyright owner, J. Bridgers

Copyright 2013
Author Josephine Jenkins Bridgers
Publisher: Josephine Jenkins Bridgers

Imprint: Jan'na HCS/print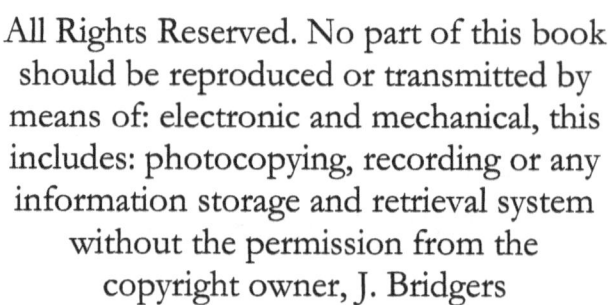

Book Covering
by Denise Sharpe

I Laughed, I Hollered by JJB

I laughed, I hollered
I laughed. I hollered. I daydreamed.
I laughed. I hollered. I was bullied.
I laughed. I hollered. I was raped.
I laughed. I hollered; I smiled to hide the tears.
I laughed. I hollered. Help me someone!
I walked away a bruised spirit spreading my seeds of Hopelessness

Beauty lies within our reach

I live my story by Josephine j. Bridgers

I live my story
I walk the steps that others before me
bedded down
So that I would have opportunities
That is what silence my tears and "lift me
up" beyond my means
Even though I sit amidst the chaos
I rise beneath the dust that falls beneath my
feet
I Rise to become not just a woman of needs
to a person of self-worth.
I think about the vision of dreams lifted up
on the bellies of slave's while
Giving nutrition to the master's child
They were lifted by the spirit of hope
I Rise from being a mortal woman to a
woman that doesn't behold to doubt or
Fear
I live my story not for the world to embrace
but for all those runaway slaves who
refused to be whipped or chained anymore.
I live my life in remembrances of the
Underground Railroad because without their
Hearts opened, doors would remain closed

I live my story for the ones hidden in the wilderness but wake up in the dawn of the night,
Thinking about, it could have been their sons or daughters killed by gun violence and Senseless killings
Yes, I know you are hurting but "you are not alone"
Rise up from the fear that bounds men saying you can't
and replace it with, I can!
That is why I live my story
To inspire others because without
A path opened up for me,
There would be no stories
There would be no dreams

Author's note:

I was inspired to write *I Live My Story* because so many times we lose insight about the struggles that came before us. People rose beyond their thinking and leaned on a higher being to get them through their trials and tribulations. That's why we must invite the dreams that were within their eye sights to continue.
We mustn't forget!

Child Speak Out speaks to the heart; my name is Jamey L. Wilkins; I'm a poet, author, songwriter, rapper, etc. Included in this book, Child Speak Out are some of my finest work. My aunt, Josephine Bridgers gave me the opportunity to contribute by being a part of this enlightening piece of literature. Child Speak Out by J. Bridgers will give you a sneak preview of this young girl's struggles to overcome a failed system while dealing with every abuse unimaginable. But through it all, her relentless strength helped her to overcome and forge a road amidst the chaos to find her way out of darkness to dream dreams.

Being incarcerated for 16 years has permanently scarred me. It left me with an indescribable sense of guilt. Not from what I did but from what I failed to do.

I was not able to have a hand in raising my child for one but the wound that will haunt me forever is the fact that I was not able to be there for my ailing mother as she suffered from cancer.

This created an insatiable desire to be the successful man I knew my mother would want me to be. I wanted her to witness me taking the necessary steps in order to achieve this because throughout my incarceration all she heard or knew was that I stayed in the hole (segregation) for one thing or another.

Which was a fact. I ended up spending nine and a half years straight in solitary confinement, no lunch breaks. Averaging over 23 hours a day stuck inside of a concrete box.

This type of long term lock up has been considered a form of psychological torture but I refused to fall victim to the mental strain that made so many succumb. I countered the weight by building the strength of my brain. Constantly learning things to occupy my time exercised my brain to the point where I was able to bear that weight.

I can't say that it hasn't changed me, hurt me, or adversely affected me, but I can defiantly scream that it did not break me.

While in that health inspection failing sarcophagus I began to study my history. I learned about the major religion, the bible, The Quran, psychology, philosophy etc. Everyone from Genghis

Khan to Malachai Z. York. From Hannibal, the black war general, to Marcus Garvey. The black panther party and the differences between capitalism, socialism, communism and anarchy. Which led to a life of rebellion. With this knowledge from behind a steel door I organize the largest hunger strike ever in the N.C. prison system and persuaded a team of anarchists to come to central prison and protest outside of our windows.

This zeal to somehow make the world acknowledge my existence also helped me learn the law. With this knowledge I took on the attorney's general office in an excessive force case against the advice of seasoned lawyers and ended up setting a precedent for the fourth circuit when I took my case to the highest court in the land and winning a unanimous verdict.

Even though this guaranteed me a place in every lawbook that was and will be published concerning prisoner's rights I did not consider this the type of success I wanted. Once I accomplished this impossible feat all the lawyers that had advised me against pursuing this case came back to represent me in a retrial.

This is when I got my first taste of how corrupt and unjust the system actually was. I won at trial. The jury concede that my civil rights were violated then awarded me a total of 99 cents. The judge threw me an extra penny to round it off to a dollar! In other words, the same civil rights that my forefathers died for were barely worth a dollar to them.

From that point on I saw through the illusion of justice. I dug deeper into every book I could find in search of an explanation. After my mother passed and I was not allowed to go to her funeral the last bit of
respect I had for the system evaporated. The true intent of the system was not to rehabilitate me but to debilitate me. This revelation hardened me and formed an igloo over my heart. I no longer cared. Then my aunt Josephine helped me channel this pent-

up anger and release it in my music poetry and books. She reminded me that I still had a daughter that needed me and that was my saving grace because only my daughter had the power to melt my frozen heart and inspire me to utilize my talent and tell my story.

Grown Folk Love by Jamey Wilkins

Sun kissed
Tan, Brown, Ebony, Bronze
In my arms forever is where you belong
Eyes like bottomless pit so deep
Skin chocolaty rich so sweet
My hand in your hand
Your hand in mine
Skipping along barefoot
Through the sands of time
Chasing the fading sun
Until we are deceased
Knowing you made it safely
Is the only way I'll rest in peace
When I placed you before me
I knew what it was
More than just infatuation
This is Grown Folk Love
Sun kissed
Bronze, Tan, Brown, Ebony
Only God can create a bond so heavenly
Your hair
Though not the longest
Is still without a doubt
The strongest
Your rib is my rib
My rib is yours
In you I found peace
After so many wars

Your touch alone
Can ease my storms
Whether a peck on the cheek
Or just a squeeze on my arm
Ever since that first time
I knew what it was
This aint no play-play stuff
Naw, this Grown Folk Love
Sun kissed
Ebony, Bronze, Tan, Brown
A smile creases my face
Whenever you come 'round
A blessing
Our connection
Of perfection
I'm your Adam
You're my Eve
On cruise control
You're my speed
No mile can separate us
No trial can deflate us
You are joy to the tenth degree
I can't explain what you've meant to me
As soon as you accepted me
I knew what it was
Not lust not a crush
Naw, this is Grown Folk Love
Sun kissed
Ebony, Bronze, Tan, Brown

This is A Heartfelt Story

It will touch your heart!

CONTENTS

About the Author 15..

....

Acknowledgement 16..

Introduction: 17...

Foreword 22..

Chapter One: 28..

Chapter Two 34...

Chapter Three 43...

Chapter Four 51..

Chapter Five 60...

Chapter Six 72 ……………………………………

Chapter Seven 84……………………………………

Chapter Eight 92…………………………………………

Chapter Nine 105…………………………………………

Chapter Ten 109…………………………………………

Chapter Eleven 122…………………………………………

Epilogue 153……………………………………

Poets Empowerment Pages 159…………………………………………

"Love is what we strive to have and give to others along their paths"

Let a child be a child!

A Child's Dream

Sweet honey drops of hope penetrate my heart,
Captivated by dreams of flowers,
Relaxing their blooms in the breeze of the winter.
Icicles filled with sweet plums melt in my mouth,
As I think of a brighter day, a day filled with shadow boats.
Bubbles of waves interrupt my thoughts with pleasurable dreams of milky- way stars.
Sparkles of rain scattered the ground with pleasurable things all around.
Perilous days of scattered dreams suddenly interrupt my daily routine.
My pursuit for happiness I continue to surrender,
To the many challenges I attempt to achieve. As every year passes, a penny of hope remains because of the graceful beauty that is part of a child's dream.

Hush Little Black Boy by JJB

Hush little black boy, daddy just gone for a stay.
But, look over yonder momma, didn't you say
that yesterday
Hush little black boy, sleep is not far away
But momma how can I sleep, when there's work
to be done and bills to be paid
Hush little black boy, one day your daddy will
return. But momma, you never told me where he
done gone? My feet are burden down. I fetched
the cows their straw.
Gave the chicken their corn. Day after day,
daddy is still gone. But momma, there are still
things I got to fetch before my work is done.
Hush little black boy it's time to go to sleep
But mamma, my back is sore from chasing the
cattle and the sheep.
Hush little black boy just close your eyes,
but momma, why did daddy leave us without
clothes or supplies? Hush little black boy,
everything will be alright. But why
every night I heard the plip plop of your tears,
that what kept me awake.
But God soften my burdens, he provided
raindrops to embrace me as a friend while I
tugged on to my pillow, falling fast to sleep. This
I promise you mommy,
until the day I'm no more, I will become the
man my father never was, so please mommy dry

up your tears! Don't cry! God heard your pain because Tomorrow I'm done being a child! Mommy I will make sure you have breakfast and do all my chores. I will walk beside you not behind you, because God gave me the strength to walk inch by inch until I can walk a mile.

To make a change, we mustn't forget the past

About the Author

Josephine J. Bridgers graduated from Edgecombe Community College with an Associate Degree in Medical Assisting. She loves people and strives to see the best in everyone. She loves writing poems and she enjoys creating poetic masterpieces with her gift of words. A native of Tarboro N.C., she believes that passion drives us to achieve the best; not giving up is the best formula for success. She believes that we are better than the script that was paved before us. We have the power to correct the wrongs and set a standard by saying to the ones struggling, I come to you my brother/sister to help you gain empowerment. Reach out my friend and secure your dream!

Acknowledgements

This revision of Child Speak Out! has required me to dig deep and draw out the pain within. Through all the rough roads, my family has helped lighten my burden, and for that I thank them. These are the people that helped make this book possible: Kimberly Hill, Bertha Haynes, Mary Hinton, Bettie Harrison and Arthur Foster.

Special Thanks to: Calvin Bridgers, Michael Hill, Lillian Jenkins and Larry Hill

Also, **I would like to thank, my nephew, Jamey Wilkins, a gifted poet in this amazing collection.**

Introduction

This book is based on a true story, but due to the unambiguous and explicit details, the names have been changed and some events have been modified to protect the identities of the people involved. The title *Child Speak Out* was chosen because some of the events were so mind-boggling they caused periods of silence. There were disastrous events around every corner, but the young child in this story lived through all the misfortunes and mayhems and they strengthened her character. The book was written as a healing process for others with similar stories, to legitimize their complaints and let them know others have walked down this same path. Some of the things described in this book might be disturbing, but they were a way of life. This book walks you through every aspect of Josie's, the main character's, life. Experiencing every type of abuse imaginable, Josie relies on inner strength to fulfill her purpose.
***

Many people experience abuse; whether it's mental or physical, the damages of abuse can have a lasting effect. *Child Speak Out* details accounts that actually happened. Josie's troubles proceeded to follow her into her adult life. Some of the events might seem difficult to swallow; nevertheless, it's her story. There are added details to give these events a theatrical effect. Most touching in this amazing story is the child's

mother. Even though she was battling depression, she was a pillar of strength for all who met her. This amazing woman makes comeback after comeback to reclaim her family. So many people would have given up but she didn't, not Della. She was zealous in her efforts to take back what was lost. With drive and determination, a person can overcome any obstacle put in their way. It is difficult not to be affected by the events that took place in this book. In the case of Josie, she had a gift in the making. . . the power of just believing and dreaming. This allowed Josie to look beyond the thin veneer of disguise and accept every person as a prolific (productive) individual. Daydreaming and seeing things through picturesque sceneries have allowed Josie to focus on friendship and encouragement. These are some of the ways that Josie visualized her world as a child and later as she matures into an adult.
***

Josie experienced mental illness firsthand with a mother battling to overcome her mental state. People suffering from issues related to mental illness have two strikes against them because mental illness is considered the crazy illness. Don't laugh! How many times has someone called you crazy! Imagine having someone in your family suffering from depression. It is impossible to escape the stigmas attached to this illness.

Look! There goes a crazy. It's just a fact; it's common for someone to say.

Now, picture a young girl or boy having to deal with name-calling because one of their parents is suffering from mental issues. Even though, young, a child knows when something is not quite right. Since this disease usually goes untreated, the person sick usually goes undiagnosed before help is available. By that time, the mentally ill person has caused much heartbreaking damage to his or her family; it is heartbreaking. There's clearly a blocked wall of communication and no repair is in sight.

***

Even the word *depression* excites controversial comments. If a depressed person is treated, he can perform without any hesitation and be a productive individual. Still, people consider them the lost souls, the ones society has frowned upon hoping that they will vanish. When a child faces these obstacles, it takes all the strength in the world to cover up for their family's imperfections. Josie's family was no exception to the rule. Today, mental illness issues have plagued so many lives and made many housebound. With mental illness on the rise, finding a solution should be a high priority, but with high budget cuts, no wonder there are so many sick people roaming the streets. Since mental illness is prevalent in some families, it is crucial to find a balance to help heal the minds of those that are besieged with this disease. Help is necessary because, without help, there is increasing stress and life becomes more horrendous. For the main character, sanity and insanity are only a moment away. There's a slogan

that the main character could apply to this story: *Life is hard but living and loving are extremely harder.* ***
It is hoped that this book will help the millions of survivors with parallel situations to heal their wounds and know their pain is justifiable. If you are struggling from depression or some other illness, it is hoped that this intimate disclosure will help you find inner peace. This is a story based on a young girl's need for stability in her immediate family. People said her mother was depressed; she could have been bipolar or affected by another disease. Whatever the disease (if there was one), she couldn't cope with the abuse her husband inflicted on her. Later, it *was* discovered that she suffered from a form of depression, which is a serious biological disorder. This was combined with her husband's unfaithfulness; so what woman who had to put up with all of this would be sane! Since, life requires a lot of tolerance, some passages detail abuse associated with trusted officers, only to show that even with law enforcers there are breakdowns in the system. If we remain silent, this kind of behavior will be swept under the rug. Only if we stand firm, our voices will be heard.

***

Unforeseen events occurred before this book was completed. Mayhems, such as the unexpected deaths of loved ones, seemed to target the main character, but determination kept her grounded. Reading this book will help you see that the title in front of a person name is not relevant. A title doesn't make a person. It's the character that holds the remote. Today, people sometimes base judgment on a person's title, but the character that thrives within is what matters. **Growing up in the South, Josie had to fight for survival. There were so many down moments in her life because in the South, there were so many restrictions. Not giving up, Josie fights to recover from poverty that besieged her family.**

Child Speak Out will clearly show, that even with odds against you, you alone have the power to mold your life. You can use the abuse as stepping-stones or you can let them cripple you.

This book takes you on a ride to educate. The journey doesn't stop at the end of the book; its length depends on you.

Foreword

"A lot of people prefer fantasy over reality. These poems distributed throughout this book are not for them. There are no butterflies or rainbows here just the stark depictions of life that express how we really feel beneath the carefully constructed veneer. Let me give you a peek inside the mind and hearts of the hood, from both a male, a female' perspective, from the eyes of the corner politician, the incarcerated philosopher, the abused mother and the quiet revolutionary. The "truth hurts" and my goal is to translate the physical pain and emotional turmoil into words."

By Jamey L. Wilkins

Da Okey Doke by Jamey L. Wilkins

Who was it that said the definition of insanity?

It's doing the same thing and expecting a different result

It seems we are psychologically doomed

Because we'd still be called crazy if we revolt

Face it, once again we've fallen for da okey doke

The old banana in the tailpipe

When will we open our eyes and see

That a broken boat will never sail right

They tell us we can protest as long as it's peacefully

Claim they listened to every word we shouted

Then turn around and do what they were going to do anyway

Absolutely nothing about it

We have to be history's biggest bunch of fouls

The laughingstock of the planet

Racism, injustice we say we can't stand it

Yet when we become victims of it all we do is withstand it

The fact of the matter is the deck is stacked

The game is rigged let's put it out in the open

We've been duped it's simple mathematics

Those who are outnumbered can always be outvoted

So the laws reflect and protect

The interests of those that make them

What, you thought it was a coincidence

That blacks are always the ones who seem to break them?!

Nope that's the okey doke the political sleight of hand, we are intentionally avoiding the obvious.

That for the future to realistically change

Resistance must start with us

We may have been outsmarted fed outright lies

Left out to dry and outgunned

But if we invest in ourselves and stop doing the same things

Then we won't have the same outcome.

Let's stop being insane. Stop being in chains

Stop being so passive

Start protecting our own, start trusting each other

Start teaching ourselves, start being proactive

Take the initiative, grab hold of the reins

That fasten to the bit in the mouth of destiny

Then our posterity will thrive in an environment

Free from the fear of a premature death that is unless we keep

Falling 4 da okey doke!

I was there by Jamey L. Wilkins

When the burden was more than a normal person could bear, my mother's shoulder never bent, I know cause I was there From a victim of abuse, to abuse me you wouldn't dare
She got stronger with every setback, I remember cause I was there. When at the Kingdom Hall she noticed someone falling asleep in the chair, a sharp pinch got their attention, I felt it cause I was there
When every cent went to bills and rent, her check had nothing to spare
My momma found a way to feed us, I know cause I was there
When a switch or belt was unnecessary punishment could come with a stare, in the midst of some kind of trouble
Yep, you guessed it; I was thee
But when she needed a kiss and hug for me to show
her how much I care
She wasn't able to receive them cause out of all times,
I wasn't there

Guaranteed Victory Jamey L. Wilkins

Why fight if I can't win
In order to keep living I must give in
But life is more than simply breathing
Life is based on the principle of freedom
So, accepting abuse to avoid death
Is in effect killing yourself
Why fight if I can't win
That depends on what defines win
If it is suffering, confined to dreams
Or causing others to be limited to these things
Then to get that victory I'd refuse
So, if I aint trying to win, how can I lose?

Chapter One
Josie

I was born Janice J. Bridges. My parents, Ed and Della Bridges, were both from a big family. As I look back, it seemed my life was normal. I was the second daughter in a line of eleven children. My mother had two sons prior to meeting my dad. Life at our home was normal--at least from my point of view. Growing up in the early 60s was a challenge because my mother had one child right after another. Eva, Dana and I, the older kids, didn't want any more siblings because we felt there were already enough.

Ed-man and Della

Ed-man—that's what people called him—was slim built, with a raging temper that few had the pleasure of knowing about and a foul mouth that seemed to be saturated with words not fit to grace the presence of young kids. Ed-man was an alcoholic that misused his authority especially on his own family; it seemed all he did was make us cry. Was this his passion in life? However, this was the life my father knew, a life of torture for all who loved him. My mother was the opposite. Della had a curvy figure that caused my father to peak high on the jealousy side. Della was very loving and caring but suffered from depression. Della was beautiful: her skin was evenly tanned brown with stunning bone structures. There were times when I would stare at her for hours; secretly, I wished some of the beauty she possessed would rub off

on me. But, nevertheless, I was proud to be in the company of my mother because she was very strong despite her illness. Someone told me Mother had a nervous breakdown before I was born. There is no certainty of that. All I know is that she was an amazing woman.
***

This long journey began in a small city in North Carolina. One evening, as I recalled, Daddy yelled, "Come here" from the front of the house. Eva, Dana and I ran hurriedly to the front room where Daddy was sitting facing Momma. "Got some treats for you kids," he smiled, handing Eva and me a quarter. He only gave Dana two dimes. "You've been some good kids," he continued to say." Now, go to the store," he ordered. Dana was very hesitant; she kept watching my father, but my behind was already thinking about the candy this little piece of change would buy me. Eva and I ran off skipping and singing.

When we got back to the house, Momma was crying, and blood was dripping from her face. The pungent odor disturbed me. Cynical, my blood started to boil! Not again! Can't he at least come home without whipping my dear mother's ass? My mother was so devoted to my father. She saw past the burn on his face due to a fire when my father was little. Her love for him was genuine. Why did she put up with his rage? Why? I questioned myself repeatedly. Nevertheless, I became very good at running away from certain problems dealing with Mr. Ed and his rage.

Life was hard because my father's drinking kept our family running and crying. One of his favorite habits was practicing what words to use to curse my mother out.

Words like bitch, whore and other disturbing words; these were low class words that he could pronounce.

"Come here, you bitch. "Come here, whore." What person does that? But Mr. Ed was different.

Damn and B*** these words rang in my eardrums every day. Eventually, those words became a part of my vocabulary. It was not a surprise because children pick up what their parents do.

Ha! Mr. Ed even used profanity that wasn't in the English language. But I'm not here to focus on the cursing part in this book.

Every night my father came home drunk. Why! I guess to appease his gigantic ego and to saturate pain on his entire family. He knew how alcohol made him act, but Father got some thrill out of torturing everyone in the house and he truly succeeded in his mission.

Oh, it's time to run. . .. Slam! It was the bogeyman, skinny, drunk and filled with pure tee hell; it's Mr. Ed. Slam! Aw, here we go again!

Damn! Damn!

Della can't you do anything right! Didn't I see a man running out the back door when I came in? He screamed at my mother.

"No, Ed!" She replied.

But his rage simply didn't stop there. It was party-time, time to run.

Oh my!

Okay, no time to think. My skinny butt needs to add some space before I get a lick in my face.

"Della," he yelled! "Come here!"

Didn't I tell you not to do this? That's all right, I'm gonna give you something to make you think. I ain't no joke, you b*** I sat in the corner frozen in time, afraid to speak and afraid to cry. Then one day, Daddy snapped for sure. He was totally drunk, and it seemed like he was hallucinating, struggling to make it up the road. Boy did Mr. Ed look crazy. The sight of him caused me to panic. What's that? Pee was coming down my legs again, oh boy. Why did this man cause me so much pain? But my thoughts seemed to be sidetracked: What's in his right hand? "Oh no! Don't Daddy, I yelled out, but it was too late. Arrrr, you children get on my damn nerves," Daddy yelled! "Be quiet!" By that time, less than a second, Dad's rage had peaked: he threw an ax, right in the middle of where Eva, Dana, and the rest of the children were playing.

Bang! The ax hacked through the wood on the wall, embedding in the siding of our house. It hit the wall, missing one of my siblings, Eva, only by an inch. Boy was I scared! Dana, Eva and I ran. At that point, everyone had to fend for him or herself. Sitting in my private space, pee started to run down my legs again.

Help! Help me! Please God! As I looked up at the sky, I asked, "How could this just happen, God! I'm only a little girl, can't you give me another Daddy? Afterward, my father, Mr. Ed, would buy us Graham Crackers and drinks. Boy, I wiggled my toes and I ate, to me, all was forgiven. What a perfect life I thought.

Mr. Ed's ire usually happened late at night when he went out drinking with his buddies. Daddy always came home from his drinking spree smelling like raw eggs. The smell was beyond reasoning for a young child, but I endured it with no arguments. But this one night, it was worse. In a drunken stupor around nine or ten o'clock, Dad tumbled into our bedroom. The aroma of his breath made me want to vomit. He bypassed each of our beds, yelling and screaming profanities into our ears. "Wake up, you bitch; f*** you," he ranted on. He was foaming around his mouth like a mad dog. The next day, Mr. Ed acted polite, never voicing the commotions of the night before. Such a pathetic loser!

In life you learn whatever tools are necessary to function; the tool used for me was sucking up to my father. My hair was the longest; he treated me the best. My behind got fewer
beatings than the rest; wasn't I blessed. That's what my sisters thought. Secretly, all wasn't well with my daddy and me; I detested him. I hated all that he stood for; he wreaked his bad temper on those in the home who were at his mercy. But, if I was bigger and stronger, it would be pay back for that skinny weasel. His presence made his existence painful. What child wants to see their family in chaos all the time? In my mind, I

dreamed of pleasurable thoughts about how happy our life would be without my father. Loathing him made my life easy to digest. Cursing, shouting and fighting all the time, this broke us down. Didn't the stupid man realize we were children and our independence were just forming? Just thinking about how father behaved, made my temper escalate. Recently, after speaking to my oldest sister about this, she was astonished. "Josie," she said, "I thought, you enjoyed the attention from Dad."

"No, Eva, think! Did I look happy? A person's survival mode kicks in when survival is at stake."

During the early stages of my life, my parents, Ed and Della, continued to have more kids. Our house became a Cracker Jack box, and there was not enough room to stretch out and blossom. Dana, Eva, and my other siblings barely had enough room to move. Our bedroom included two beds per room with three siblings per bed; it was normal in our house. Most of the time, I woke up with a toe or foot in my mouth. "Sleep on your side, please!" I yelled, after I woke up one morning, imagining food in my mouth. Oh no, it was someone's toe!

Chapter Two

Love, Lust, Discipline, the Look, the teachers I encountered and Xmas

In some minute way, Ed really loved Della, even though his actions dictated the opposite. On rare occasions, Mr. Ed displayed affection by kissing Della, but after Mom saw us kids staring, she would make Daddy stop. "Don't you see the kids", Della would say?
Well, Della and Ed always made time for sex. Some say it's "what love is all about." It seemed that all my parents did was stay in the bedroom.
        Stop!
How can you even think about bringing any more children into the world when all Mr. Ed did was fight and look at those nasty girlie magazines that were distributed nicely under his bed. In the magazines there were women wearing nothing but skimpy outfits. Bam! Sexual beings just jumped off the pages. On rare occasions, I saw only men showing their unforgettable. Girl, it was exciting.
  What's that! Genitals!
After secretly looking at the pictures, things seemed to happen. What was happening to me? After all, I'm just a little girl. But my god, the temperature is getting hotter!

Discipline

Discipline was no issue in our family. The children were usually disciplined with a switch or belt. Whelps were so common on Dana's, Eva's and my bodies that we thought it was a second piece of clothing. Nobody complained about this little minor thing. It was Mr. Ed, as he liked to be called, who usually did the beating. Ooh!

Mr. Ed would get out his switch, Wow! It seemed like the beatings lasted forever. Slowly the belt left my father's waist then in slow motion the sound of hits was heard throughout the house. Eva and Dana had nerves. The hits seemed to bounce off their little tiny bodies. They were both tiny, but they elevated high because of their courage. They both seemed to have strength way beyond their years. How do you think scary cat came into existence? I created it. Perspiration started popping when dad called my name, "Josie, come here," when it was my turn to get the belt. A noise came from my mouth that even frightened me. Help me! I can't take this no more God!

While screaming, "Stop! Stop!" when Daddy whipped me, it seemed like there were thousands of people whipping my tail, not this skinny little man that wasn't big as a tadpole. Sometimes, I would go in the bedroom that I shared with my sisters and pull my panties down and examined the bruises on my butt; even though my butt was black, there were red bruises on it. I nursed the wounds like the nurses did in real life. Just the sight of a belt—Whoa! Whoa! was enough to make me cry. Daddy beat me until there were welts, because without welts, he thought he hadn't done anything.

The Look!

Parents used this as a secret weapon, The Look! The Look represented all things: fear, love, anger, joy etc. But when my father gave us The Look, it put fear in our hearts especially mines. When he sat you down and gave us that look, we knew what was about to happen.

Along with dealing with my father, there was a bully in Elementary school that gave me the look; but this was a different kind of look. The Look from him meant, hand over your lunch or I beat your tail! So, I gave in, because my tail was worth more than a bologna sandwich or was it?

Elementary school was no cup of tea, because there was a bully who always ate my lunch every day; his name was James Brown. His presence caused me trepidation. "Give me your lunch!" he would say; fearing James, I would give him my neatly wrapped crackers with peanut butter and jelly. Sometimes I gave him, my neatly wrapped bologna sandwich.

One day, James Brown got bold and couldn't wait for lunch. He went straight to the area where the treats were kept and started eating. Oh, this time James made a serious boo-boo. Ms. Pink glanced at the section where James was throwing down and said, "Are you eating already, James?" One brave little boy, named Rob, yelled out, "That's my lunch, Ms. Pink." Ms. Pink yelled and yelled. "No wonder everyone in class is afraid of you, James. You are nothing but a big bully. If you breathe wrong from here to eternity, your butt will get it; you hear me!"

In the 60s, teachers could beat the mess out of their students and the power behind those hits was felt for days. So many students had sore butts, even some had marks from the hits, but no one called Social Services, and Child Protective Services didn't exist then.

After that incident, Mrs. Pink watched James more closely to make sure he wasn't eating anyone else's lunch. Our mother didn't know what was going on. She didn't know the bully ate my lunch every day; she only knew that, at home, food didn't stand a chance.

The three eldest girls were very close in age; if we had any sense, we could've gotten together and beaten that bully, but our thinking wasn't that advanced.

Running home one day, Dana, Eva and I yelled, "Momma! Momma! Michael, Sandy, Judy, Mary and John are trying to fight us!" Stomping back and forth, my mother was steaming out of her nose. Okay, now mother gave us the look! She told us if we didn't get our butts back out there and fight, the beating we would get from her would be much worse. Dana, Eva and I looked at each other as we understood Momma's feelings. Then like soldiers, we marched back and gave those awful kids the fight of their lives. To my surprise, we won the battle that day. From that day on, I stopped running and started fighting back.

Some of my memories of my earlier years were euphoric. One of my favorite memories was when my mom would bring us lunch every Friday. Everyone had their own private bag of goodies: a bologna sandwich, vanilla wafers, an apple and a drink. The lunch was so delicious. Oh boy! My mouth waters thinking about it. Life was so simple then, when burdens were placed on the backs of adults and delicacy of food was savored for a later surprise.

Likes and Dislikes of My Teachers

Have you ever wondered what happened to some of your teachers? Well, let me think . . . there was one teacher or misguided soul who was not fit to teach any kids. Yes, yes, she was Ms. Johnson. Just thinking about her irritates me. Yep, she taught elementary school. This one teacher was just a nightmare because she would give the light skinned-students better grades. Trust me, it's the truth. One of Ms. Johnson's favorite students was Bettie. Bettie was the epitome of beauty in Ms. Johnson's eyes. What teacher gives better grades for just being light skinned? Well, Ms. Johnson did. She seemed so awestruck with skin color that it was ridiculous. Working in a field that was supposed to mold young minds, this teacher provided another obstacle for Blacks. Molding and shaping our minds should've been Ms. Johnson's purpose, but sadly, she didn't care about the negative impact she had on our young lives. What was a little chocolate child like me to do? Ha!

Did I stand a chance? No, because my skin was Black. I was introverted and being silent was my way of dealing with her prejudices. The persona Ms. Johnson displayed in the street was different from the persona displayed in the classroom, but she was evil. To me, it was just another obstacle, which caused me to retreat into a world of make believe. In this make-believe world, I was a princess and my subjects obeyed my utmost desires. Ms. Johnson should have had more compassion, especially since she knew that racism was a part of the South's agenda, and the stench of its aftermath was thrust in our face every day. But she just added to the flame; sadly, she didn't have a clue.

Like anything in life, there were several teachers that were great; one was a young male teacher, named Mr. Blackman. He was striking, just what I envisioned a perfect man to be: dark, black and handsome. Mercy me! He had it going on. He was just gorgeous! Looking up from my seat, I would stare at this man for hours.

Mr. Blackman was from the old school. He disciplined his students severely, especially, the boys who always acted up in his class. One of his favorite lines were, "What are you smiling about with your pearly whites?" One day outside, one little boy student struck Mr. B's last nerve. Mr. Blackman's eyebrows rose; he was mad and without thinking, he kicked Jackie in the butt.

The next day, in marched Jackie's mother ready to fight. Jackie's mother couldn't take a joke because Mr. B was only playing. He wasn't trying to cause harm to anyone. But Jackie's mother was ready to fight; she was built like a man; and what was that in her pocket book? It looked like real boxing gloves. Jackie's mother temper met the teacher at the door and she cursed and cursed. She ran the teacher outside-- this woman was ready to battle! Jackie's mother was gigantic: she looked like she could've wrested a wrestler and won. This the first time Mr. Blackman looked like he was about to panic, but the saga continued until the principal came.

Ha, ha

      Oh!

This was exciting; we watched the madness with horror and anticipation. It was like a Cowboy and Indian movie; Jackie's mother was trying her best to hit the teacher, but he kept ducking. It was so funny. Man, oh man! Can you imagine your teacher and a parent running around the classroom today? Guns would be fired instead of fists. But, Mr. Blackman was an excellent teacher; his method of teaching was very effective, and he was a no-nonsense type of guy. Aw, he personified a perfect specimen. He was my black chocolate hulk. Oooh! Nothing could sway me from admiring Mr. Blackman! I get a bud just thinking about this man.

Christmas

Christmas was the best holiday of the year. On Christmas Day, you could smell cakes and pies . . . the aroma was smelled throughout our home. During Christmas the air was filled with anticipation, the smell of the trees, and the sound of children laughing; these were moments that will envelope my mind forever! But in our family, we didn't get fancy gifts like computers or battery-operated games. Christmas was simple with more focus on the family. Life back then produced some of my fondest memories. I remember that one year, I received a beautiful doll. Love it!
That very doll remained in my toy chest until I was in ninth grade. These were times when the world wasn't so complicated. It was the season when Eva, Dana and I, the three oldest girls, would go in the woods before Christmas day and look for a fantastic Christmas tree. The smiles on our faces were priceless when we found one. Marching on with an axe in one hand and a wagon in the other, we chopped down the best tree. It was wonderful. What children wouldn't be proud of this? We heard all the beautiful birds; it was euphoric. The woods were filled with all the nature beauty, small water ponds, exotic plants, colorful birds and insects scattered around the wild flowers like a paradise described in the bible.

When we went home, we made paper decorations for our gigantic Christmas tree. Wow! It gives me goose bumps just thinking about it. Most children today get everything they want for Christmas. But back then, Christmas was a time when the best was served; this was the dress up holiday. Momma would give us pork chops because this delicacy was reserved only for Dad, but Christmas was an expectation to the rule! Children appreciated simple gifts and the look on our faces . . . Ahhh, it was priceless. Christmas today is not the same because no one seems to truly appreciate this magnificent holiday. When I was young, everyone would gather up their toys and go outside to play; it was a sense of pride, pride in having a family; pride in knowing there was love everywhere. This day was only for kids; this day would always be engraved in my heart forever. Today, children get computers and electric games, which were unheard of in my generation. Most of the children today stay inside with their computers, it takes the spirit out of Christmas. This is not what Christmas is about. Nowadays, it even seems gloomy at times.

Now people talk about me time, hell the only time we had me time back then, was when it was time for us to go to sleep.

Chapter Three

Innocent Years or Where they

Childhood friends weren't an issue because we had each other. Some of our friends' names were: Stephan, Randy, Taylor, Candy Ginger and Gloria. Gloria was stunning, with long floating hair; she was the embodiment of beauty. Secretly, I envied her. Why was Gloria's hair so long? Her skin was so white. Was she really a little white girl? I thought secretly. Back then, if a person resembled whiteness, man, oh man, you were considered to be in the in-crowd, one of the beautiful people. This was considered the epitome of beauty. Now get mad, but this is one of the pitfalls of society, and society dictates what beauty is, not me. Don't ask me why, but if you did, one answer would be that the lighter you are, the better you are accepted in society and, sadly, it is still true today. Ain't that a shame. But if you watch the videos seen on TV, you rarely see darker women dancing on them. And the odd thing is that most of the black artists don't represent their own, which is odd to me because we are low on the scale of respect as it is. What do you think?

Getting back to my childhood . . . with every day, there was another escapade. Most of the time, I spent my time daydreaming about a prince rescuing me from my dungeon, >>>>>>>>

this house of horror. My prince would set me free, free to be a child, free to enjoy the delicacy of a variety of food. Free to travel the world and see things in the mind of a child.

But for fun time, there was a little boy that frequented our house who was a little depraved (corrupted). Stephan was his name and he lived next door. Stephan would expose his little private part every evening, just like a clock, as he did his little funny dance in the window. Excited, all the neighbors' children would gather outside anticipating his next performance. We thought it was hilarious.

        Ha! Ha!
What's that? He was holding it in the window.
        Oh my, it was his genitals,
Stephan lacked inhibition, but he was quite entertaining to the other kids in the neighborhood. Stephen certainly speeded up my hormones, if I had any at the time. Why did Stephan do that? Who cares! But for the kids in the neighborhood, it was a treat. Enough of that! A thrill comes over me just thinking about it. Coming from a large family, we lacked the commodities that a smaller family had. One commodity was a TV. This didn't stop Dana, Eva, Dora and me. We used as our advantage the ability to peep in the windows of our neighbors to watch different shows at night. The boys sometimes opened their curtains, so we could see things on TV. They were our best friends and, secretly, my thoughts drifted back to James, this

little boy. Man, he ignited my fire--if there was a fire at my age. James was tan- brown with the most adorable face that kept me staring at him for hours. Ouch! I almost swallowed my tongue, thinking about James. Nevertheless, the boys were our closest friends.

Dana, Eva and I occupied our thoughts with games: hopscotch, jump rope and the kissing game. Back then, those were the games of choice. No one complained of being bored like they do today. Even with all the high-tech gadgets developed for young children to play with today, still they complain about being bored. Children never got bored in the 60s. Back then, there was always something to do. Would you believe I was so stupid that I thought that kissing would cause someone to get pregnant? Now tell me that ain't stupid. James had just kissed me. When will the baby come? Mommy never had the girlie talk so my imagination was running wild. But, I was terrified; there would be no more kissing on the cheek from now on. Then my thoughts drifted to my secret love, James. Boy, why was James so cute? My black face turned pink when James came around, was he my prince charming? Maybe James would rescue me one day from this house of horror that sucked the life out of us because of Mr. Ed.

Spring or summer, all I know is, it was hot hot! I can't remember what season it was, but for some strange reason, Dana and I decided to dip some snuff. We had seen our momma, Della, and Aunt Lay put some in their mouth and let it s simmer, taking in the favor. Momma and Auntie seemed to enjoy it so much, so we tried it. Dana got dizzy first; then my head started spinning, around and around. Instead of us holding the snuff under our tongue, we swallowed it. We never got to savor the favor because we swallowed the stuff. We got drunk as a skunk. Sick, oh boy, we were sick. We struggled to get on the bed; everything seemed to be spinning around. All I know is, I became paralyzed with fear, fear that this was my last breath, and fear I would never see my mommy again. From that day on, Dana and I swore we would never dip stuff again.

Awful! Awful! Spit! Spit!

There were so many beautiful memories of my childhood, but this one was not. Here is the story.

One beautiful bright day, Eva and I decided to go and pick some berries. While picking the berries, I reached over to get one that looked delicious. Ouch! There was a sharp pain in my foot. Looking down, I noticed blood was pouring out from my left foot. Eva, Eva, my foot is hurt! We both ran back home as if we had stolen something. In my room by my dresser, I spotted a plastic boot. Without thinking, I put it on my bleeding foot. Come on, I was a child, what was I pose to do? My mind wasn't thinking correctly, and for some strange reason, my head was hurting. It was like someone was knocking on top of my head; all I could do was hold my head, as I laid down. Eva came running in the house, "Josie, Josie," she yelled! "I'm in the back room," I yelled back to her. By then, blood was pouring out of my boot. Eva yelled! Girl, you did it this time. By this time my big brother came in, he yelled what have you done Josie! When he pulled the boot off my foot, there was blood everywhere. Ray's face turned red.

"Call a cab!" He hollowed to the neighbors. Momma was in the State Hospital, so Ray, my oldest brother, was the one in charge of looking after the kids. Ray took me to the hospital. It seemed like miles before we reached our destination; I was thrifting in and out, while the blood poured out everywhere.

At the hospital, the doctor put thirty or more stitches in my foot.

Ouch! Ouch! It hurt!

The pain was penetrating all the way up my leg. The doctor told me if my brother had waited any longer, my family would've been going to a funeral. Stupid and naïve, my mind didn't understand the severity of this matter.

All I remembered is that I got some candy, and it was good while I drifted into a land of make-believe.

Teenage Years

Thirteen is the magic year. But for me, it was another year of senseless episodes. On my face there were bumps everywhere; it seemed like my face was a road map that lead to my big, gigantic nose. How disgusting! Boy, did I hate my nose! It was a reminder of my genes from my dad. This one inheritance was a nightmare for me. But for some strange reason, people thought I was beautiful though. It seemed like my hormones were going crazy. Little did I know that some things that happened during my thirteenth year would eventually bring on negative memories, memories that would last me a lifetime! Melancholy memories, life, love and regrets.
Those were the innocent years; now these memories are a distant part of my past.

Out of nowhere, a close, close, relative returned. Being so naive, my stupid butt welcomed him as if I had forgotten the abuse I suffered at his hands. How could someone so close want to be with his own relative? Heinous! Well, his passion for me was like a raging bull and somewhat retarded! Bob followed me around all day. Like a sycophant, he wanted favors, so he buttered me up with flattering remarks, candy and chips, and raped me! Terrified, it was my worst nightmare. How could he? This was incest with a big Bang! Being older, he very much knew what he was doing, but lust overtook his sanity. After years of putting this behind me, now it happened again, this horrendous deed. How can anyone long for their own family member? It's Crazy! Damaged goods from the hands of their own relative . . . there are so many people facing this dilemma. What a shame. This has haunted me my entire life. He stole a part of me, because he stole my virginity. Why tell when no one would listen! Momma didn't know whom to believe. I tried to tell, but Momma was caught in the middle. Sadly, being a parent is hard! She can't be blamed for her imperfections. It's life! Then a couple of months after the rape, I went to school and my menses started. Didn't know a thing about what was going on. But when I went in the bathroom and saw my panties, for some strange reason, I thought my tail was split. No one had any conversation with me about menses. That day in that bathroom, I rubbed and rubbed, but still more blood came out. What was I to do? Then without more hesitation, I carefully unrolled tissue and lined my panties with the paper.

> *"When you communicate, the receiver receives your message"*

Chapter Four

Secrets, Lies and The Relatives who molded me

Deloris was one of my closes friends, but her life was awful. She was very petite with long hair and very stunning. Something bad had happened to Deloris though: someone had abused her, someone very close to her. But it's not my story, so ask her if you dare! It takes humor to endure hardship. What do you think? Deloris stayed with my family for about a week or two, because her life of abuse at home doubled the abuse of mine, but nevertheless, it's her story to tell. I could, however, wet your lips with only a few details and say that a family member of Deloris had abused her. Even with my daddy's acts of violence, my life was a sugar-coated candy bar compared to hers. But why did my dad always seem to come in the room naked when Deloris was around? It puzzled me. He strutted his body right in front of us. Was he stupid? We didn't want to see his ding go ling. How disgusting for a child to see! But we were used to seeing his private part, because Daddy marched around all the times, especially when we had company. Poor Deloris, this was the last thing she wanted to see. But Daddy celebrated his package with honors. Now, I'm leaving that alone. Bam!

Positive Role Model

Everyone has a favorite uncle or aunt. Mine was Uncle Jeff. When Uncle Jeff visited, Daddy was on his best p's and q's because Uncle Jeff didn't play. Every time he heard that Daddy had beaten Momma up, it wasn't long before Uncle Jeff paid us a visit. "Ed," he would say, "not trying to get into y'all business, but don't let me hear that you hit Della again. If I see any marks on her," he said, as he made a fist," I'm gonna beat you down." Ed was truly afraid of this man. The power behind Uncle Jeff's punches was enough for my daddy to rethink his eruptions. My daddy knew first-hand that my uncle meant business; father had experienced the power behind this man's fists firsthand because uncle used only one hand to hold him while the other hand was free to clap him around. During the course of my young life, Uncle Jeff made regular visit to our home but, this particular time, after sitting on the bed for what seemed like hours, my uncle thumped the bed with his fist.

Oh my!

He pulled his fist backward as if it was on fire. It was embarrassing, for there was no mattress, but only boards under the bed's frame. Uncle Jeff had a little smirky look on his face!

Ha, ha!

Guess Uncle Jeff won't do that again. Poor Uncle Jeff. He looked hurt, hurt that his sister couldn't afford decent beds for her children, a luxury his children had.

Aunt Lay

As I think back on my Aunt Lay, I remember that this woman was medium built with an authoritative voice that was very forceful.

"Dana! Eva! Josie!" It seemed that all this woman did was yell, "Come here!"

No one challenged her. Aunt Lay was a hell-raiser. If this woman could bring men to their knees, ain't that a hell-raiser. All the children trembled in her presence, even men. They didn't stand a chance. It was her voice that projected authority. Have you ever seen someone that had something that you just couldn't put your finger on? Well, Aunt Lay represented all of that. Elevating high over me, it seemed as if she was ten feet tall. Was she a monster disguised as a human? Who knows?

Nevertheless, Aunt Lay looked after my mother's children when she was gone. It was her duty, she thought. Back then, people honored family.

Aunt Lay's husband was a shadow of a man because this woman controlled every crack and hole in her house. Absolutely no one got past Aunt Lay. Uncle Roy, yes, he was a *yes* man! All I ever heard him say was 'Yes, Lay, yes, yes.' Later on I found out his dirty little secret. Uncle Roy led a double life: one very submissive, the other a molester-- mainly, boys. This, of course, was hearsay. Whether it's true or not, it depends on the source.

On the farm where my Aunt Lay lived, there were cows, chickens, pigs, horses and various kinds of garden equipment. The equipment was used to maintain the farm. Aunt Lay had the largest pigs; the pigs were given a steady supply of grain >>>>> And corn for their feeding, and this was done daily. The oldest children did most of the feeding. Some of the hogs weighed well over 200lbs. The pigs made the best barbecue. The meat was fresh with the flavor of wood that was cooked into the meat, producing a tenderizing aroma.

Tobacco was her main crop. It brought in most of the money, but it worked the heck out of us.

Eva, Dana and I helped with the chores around the farm, along with our two older brothers, Bob and Ray. Being poor was no option when we were young; we had it all--good food and patched up clothes. Now, was this a disturbing life? Yes! First hand, I got to live with craziness because my Aunt Lay performed rituals like rubbing the walls down with oil for evil spirits, while she shouted throughout the house rebuking evil spirits in the name of the Lord. I think she was speaking in tongue. What a nut cake! Now, she called my mother crazy, but who was really the crazy person?

Oh, Aunt Lay had traits that were less than perfect. This lady took violence to another level. Guns were Aunt Lay's weapon of choice. She would pull out a gun and point it without batting an eye. There was one occasion when Daddy visited. He and Aunt Lay got into a heated discussion. Can't remember what it was all about, but before he knew it, Daddy's hat was in the air and this skinny man was running for his dear life, while Auntie yelled, "I'm gonna kill you; you skinny bastard!" But this skinny little man was gone, gone out of sight!

It seemed like he was running for hours . . . away he ran from my aunt's house, the nut cake, leaving his own kids behind to deal with this crazy woman. Then, I heard a shot. Boom! It was Aunt Lay. Would you believe this woman had gotten a gun and was firing at my father?! Her rifle kicked out another shell, but by then my father was well out of sight. It was as if this man was a super hero. Bam! He was not running but flying. All I saw was a tooth pick shadow moving . . . moving far away. "Daddy come back!" we all cried out! Sadly, Daddy was gone!

During another stay at Aunt Lay's house, she showed Dana and me the fate of womanhood. "Come here," she yelled out to Dana and me. "Auntie wants to teach you about womanhood." Great, I thought. Then, Aunt Lay pulled down her underwear and showed us her red lining in her panties. Blood was dripping down her legs. It was horrible; we screamed! Aunt Lay then proceeded to tell us we would soon be experiencing this joy in a few more years. Dana and I said, no, no, we don't want to become a woman. We ran out of the room weeping, as we vomited. How disgusting! Who would be that nasty to show dirty underwear to impressionable kids? Was she crazy? Thinking back, my aunt's explosive personality prevented people from understanding her. Shortly after that event, my mother was released from the state mental illness facility. Momma resumed custody of her family. There would be no more shouting through the house like a mad woman, I thought, because my momma was the opposite of my Aunt Lay. Dana and I continued to stay at Aunt Lay's house even with Momma home from the mental facility. Why? Who knows, we were just kids. Auntie's house was a place where secrets were kept, a place where we rode horses, picked apples, played momma and daddy games and had hayrides. It was a place where abuse was unthinkable, but it happened. There were intimate relations with relatives, but we covered up, we remained silent, we obeyed every wish. A child should never experience this, but it happens. Meanwhile, Aunt Lay marched, every night through the house, speaking in tongues in the name of religion. Stump! Stump! She did this all night. It could have been my lowest period in my life because how low can a child go? Aunt Lay also drank a lot of Castor Oil, especially when she thought she was pregnant. Someone told me my Aunt Lay would've been the mother of as many children as my mother, but her homemade abortions killed any hope of that. Ah! She even gave us tons of Castor Oil when we had flu symptoms. Castor oil was the remedy for everything, my aunt thought. If only my aunt had known, she would never have gotten rid of those babies, babies that she should have had. Her life would have had more meaning; maybe Aunt Lay would have had children that really loved her. Do you not reap what you sow?

Where my aunt lived, there were hundreds of fruit trees in the back of her huge farm. She had miles and miles of land. The air was so refreshing because back then, and there were not that many pollutants around. On the farm, there were savory apples, peaches and pears; it was a child's paradise. I ventured off one day to taste the delicious fruits--there were so many choices. After eating several ripe juicy apples, I noticed a worm in the middle. Uh! There were worms throughout the apple. Wow! Did I eat a worm? There must've been hundreds of worms in my stomach; it doesn't pay to be greedy! The apples were juicy, though. Then along came my brother, Bob. "Josie, do you want a ride," he asked? Should've known my brother was bad news! Yes! Away we went! Bob drove the wagon like a maniac; he didn't stop for holes, bumps or anything. After getting on the wagon, I realized it was a huge mistake. The two horses were trotting as if they were flying; the wagon barely made it over the bumps in the road. Several times, I almost fell off, before I jumped off into a puddle of muddy water. Stupidity was my name instead of Josie. Bob was bad--there was not a good bone in his body.

My Aunt's Good Qualities and Daily Living at An Early Age

Aunt Lay was a good cook; she made homemade cakes that literally, melted in your mouth. She used cow's milk from the farm to make the best ice cream you ever tasted. The creamy mixture . . . ah, it melted in my mouth. Aunt Lay loved us in her own way, so she gets an A for her efforts. Aunt Lay was also a cat fanatic. Usually there were about five of more cats in the house at any given time. It became a little irritating. They crawled on top of everything, even when she was cooking. Sometimes I even picked out cat hairs that were in my food. Boy, I hated those little tiny creatures for a while.

There was a house about two blocks away from the farm where my Aunt Lay lived. One day, I decided to visit the little white girl who lived there. Her name was Janice. We played games, but this day in particular. Janice, the little white girl decided to wash both of our heads. After she washed her hair, her hair was still straight; then she proceeded to wash my hair, but it turned kinky. Janice put some Dippy Do on my hair; that's when I realized my hair was different from my friend's. Both of us were astonished at the differences. The grade of hair I had wasn't bad, but Janice's hair was straight. Why was it, I thought? Well, I was puzzled. Why didn't color matter to Janice and me? When you are a kid, that kind of thing is not a focus. A lesson in prejudice must be taught. Janice wasn't prejudiced because we played together daily. After all, color is only a five-letter word...

Chapter 5

**Moving, Daddy's drama, Lesson of womanhood,
Rats and Dating**

When I was eight or nine we moved to another city. Funny thing, though, my momma did not look inside the house before she moved in. Momma's brothers had told her about the house. It was a ragged shack. Plus, the man in the house had not moved out. He was a skinny, ragged looking fellow who thought for some weird reason that he would continue to live in the house with us. This was a no, no! Momma told the man he had to leave because Bony, Ed-man, my father, would come home and kill him if he continued to stay. Everything was fine until my father came home from his job on the road, doing construction, replacing highways and building bridges.

On weekends, my daddy would chase us out of the house; calling us the B word and any other words that rhyme with F***. Being naïve, I thought all children experienced this type of behavior. Running became a hobby. During the summer, we worked, starting from the ripe old age of six. The older kids worked in the fields chopping, picking cucumbers and putting in tobacco. The sun was Hot. Hot! One day I went to school, forgetting what my aunt had taught me about feminine hygiene. I heard someone in the classroom say, "What's that smell? It smells like dead fish." My mind secretly wondered, is it I? Didn't know anything about tampons or vaginal pads; rags were used to protect myself against Mr. Red every month. Oh, well, no one had taught me about this -- only the little crazy lesson I had gotten from Auntie. It was another chapter in my process of learning and maturing into a young woman. As we got older, there was a lot of bickering and fighting amongst the kids. Eva, Dana, Dora and I always chose sides. Which one of us would be on the winning side this time, I wondered! Sometimes the fights were so intense and so violent, it was a wonder that we didn't seriously hurt each other.

It was early spring, the day after a huge fight Eva and I had. Not thinking about my injured finger, I went to school. My finger was hanging on by a thread: Eva had bitten a huge chunk of it. The assistant principal approached me after someone told him about my finger. "Who did this horrible thing?" Mr. Wade asked. Afraid, as if I had done something wrong, I spoke up: "It was my sister, Eva," I said. "We had a big fight last night." That man had the most horrible look on his face, and the few hairs on his head, were sticking straight up. After hearing my side, he called my sister in for a conference. He scolded her for biting my finger. "Why did you do it, Eva? You are the oldest, you should've known better." These incidents happened repeatedly, though. After all, we were kids.

There was another incidence: Eva was outside and being picky as always, I locked her out of the house. When she came to the door, it was locked. Then for no reason at all, I started making faces at her. She forgot that there was a window. In an instant, she reached out and punched out the glass window. That's how mad she had gotten.

"Momma!" Eva yelled. "Help me!!!" Blood was everywhere. Afraid for Eva, I cried. Why couldn't I refrain from picking? What if Eva is seriously hurt? If I hadn't been so picky, Eva wouldn't have punched that big old window. Things like this were normal; someone was always doing something around our house. Kicking, biting, slapping, fighting -- that's how it was in our house.

New Home Tainted with Rats

When I was in the third grade, we moved to a smaller city. It seemed so far, far away from the larger city that we had called our home. After moving into the house Momma Della picked out, we realized that she had forgotten to check it out. We were shocked: the house was a wreck, plus there were rats everywhere. They were very truculent, even when they were in our space. These creatures were bigger than cats. I think they were field rats because they had big long whiskers. Our home was flooded with these tainted creatures. The rats would march through the house, not fearing human presence. One of my brothers, Ernie, would have a panic attack when he saw these creatures. One day, my father locked my brother in the closet. My brother screamed and screamed!

Rats were in our closet; rats were everywhere! Teaching my brother, a lesson didn't work that day. He continued to scream when he saw these unclean creatures. Nights were unbearable: the rats would jump back and forth on our beds. They acted like they were in a clique because they always did the same thing every day and night.) One night I woke up, and there was a big giant rat crawling across my face. I screamed!

"Rats!"

Teen's years

In our teen years, dancing was our favorite form of entertainment. One evening, Dana, Eva and I were having a party. We were dancing our butts off. It didn't take much for a party in those days, only Kool Aid, chips and music and the party was on. We were dancing but I guess the people stayed to long for my daddy because my father came running in the room with a shot gun. Would you believe this man even fired his gun up in the ceiling of our living room? There out of nowhere jumped several large rats. It was embarrassing; needless to say, we didn't have any company for a while. We prayed that the guys kept that secret because if they told what happened at our house, it would've been a field day at school.

Transition from elementary school to high school was very overwhelming to me. Very demure and very shy, I avoided getting up in the front of the class when we had oral assignments. The same fear I had in elementary school followed me in high school. Because of my fears, I just chose to get a bad grade instead of standing in front of the class when it came time to recite something. I literally would have palpation.

During this time, the climate in America was changing and people were interested in self-love. They were young and carefree, and marijuana was the drug of choice. On television, there were hippies with colorful outfits promoting drugs. Everyone was enjoying his or her free space. Hot pants were the new fad. Girls wore short shorts, short skirts and dresses; sometimes their unforgettable was exposed, but we had beautiful legs—ain't that what mattered? Penny loafers were also in. Boys at school would put a piece of glass where the penny was supposed to be, so they could look up the girl's dresses when they changed their classes. I walked sideways, but I still saw some boys waiting at the end of the stairs to get a look under my dress. In my social studies class one day, I wore a red mini skirt to school; the boys had a fit. That day, in social studies we had a debate; every student was asked to plead a case in front of the class. "Get up, Josie!" a crowd of boys shouted! Did they have an ulterior motive? Oh yes, my short skirt! They were mesmerized. Why? The skirt was extremely short!

More Daddies' Drama and life of a teenager dreamer

One day when two of my siblings were away, my father became very antagonistic. He was mad because my sisters were gone. One was staying with his mother and the other was staying with his brother and his wife. He began cursing me out-- it was my time to be all the b's and f's because my two sisters were gone for the summer. Since my sisters were not there, he turned his anger on me. Daddy was mad! He beat me until I had lacerations all over my body. Then I did the unthinkable in my daddy's eyes: I went and told a neighbor about how my dad had beaten me; the only thing she told me was to go back home. She seemed to be more worried about my father than me; but back then, people thought a belt was the best solution for anything. But instead of going home, I routed my butt straight to the magistrate's office and took out a warrant on Mr. Ed, my father. Due to my age, the person residing in the office filed the papers. He took into consideration the marks on my body before he made his decision. Marks covered my legs and my abdomen. The policemen picked my father up, and happiness covered my thoughts, but my joy didn't last long. Finally, my father would get what he deserved, I thought, giggling to myself. Maybe he will be gone for good. I was having fantasy thoughts of a euphoric life without my father. This was wonderful, I thought. Then after a couple of days, Momma started pressuring me to change my story; sadly, the pressure got the best of me. Giving in to pressure from Momma, I spoke up on my father's behalf. After all, he was my daddy. My daddy probably had learned his lesson I thought.

No! Would you believe that man came home raising more Hell than ever! You would think Mr. Ed would have repented; instead, he acted worse. He continued to threaten me about getting him locked up. Boy, I hated that man!

Babysitting

One day when my dad and mom were gone, Dana and I were in charge, but instead of watching our younger siblings, we did the unthinkable: we left the smaller kids home alone. Why? We did it because we got tired of them. Careless! Wow! Dana said, "Come on, Josie, let's go and visit Carolyn." "But, Dana," I said, "don't we pose to be babysitting?" "Who will know? We're not telling," Dana replied. "You right," I said. "Let's go!" The little ones will be all right, I secretly thought, so Dana and I went to my friend's house to play cards while our smaller siblings were home alone. Bad move. When Mr. Ed came home and found the younger children alone, he came fuming up the hill where we were. Girl, I was relaxed back, laughing with my friend, Cara, when this mad man walked in the door. Smoke seemed to be coming out of his nose. Mr. Ed's nose was double the size of a regular nose, and his nose hair was showing. With a switch in one hand, he hit me. Dana had spotted him and had jumped in the ditch to hide. He proceeded to beat me all the way home. Afterward, like always, he bought cookies and drinks; I was happy. Things got better when my sisters returned. At least now, I felt he could direct his frustration on them.

High School

When I was in the tenth or eleventh grade my father asked me to go with him to the store; my boyfriend, my sister's boyfriends, all of us went with him. As we walked, a man came out of nowhere; he had broken a soda bottle behind him! "Ed! Ed! Come here," the man said, coming towards us. He told my father he just wanted to speak to him a second. I didn't know what my father had done to that man, but he did something, because the man's face was burning red and his complexion was jet black. Ed, my father, told the man, "Don't you see these big young men with me; they aren't going to let anything happen to me." The man was so mad he didn't see the guys walking behind my father. Lard, my date, was huge. He was big, black and nothing but power. After all, I knew first hand, due to the fights we had. He incited fear in itself. My sisters' dates were much smaller but built. But with the drop of a hat, it would've been on. Our dates yelled back, and the man backed off. This was no isolated incidence. Daddy was a trip; he stirred up trouble so many times.

Thinking back . . . one day he had an argument with an older gentleman, and before the gentleman knew what happened, my father had hit him on the head with a guitar. Guitar strings were hanging around his neck. Bang! Bang! It was like what you'd see on TV. After he smacked the man, he flew like a bird escaping harm's way. If my daddy thought he was going to lose a fight, he would fight "by any means necessary." People called him Super Fly after that. Ed also was called Egg-Man, because he could eat a dozen hardboiled eggs, but weighed less than the average adult man, weighing the most at 155 lbs. He was around 6 feet and some inches. By the way, my father was an excellent dancer but lacked singing abilities. He was so flexible that he could do a split and jump up, jump back and rock on his knees. He performed different exercises with a rhythm that was without flaws. It's seemed at times my daddy was a rubber band because he could really move.

Daddy's singing in the Choir

Another of my father's passions was singing, but he couldn't sing. Maybe if he took singing lessons, it might have improved his voice. Nah, he just couldn't sing a lick.

Mr. Ed's singing was like someone beating dogs. When I was in high school my father started singing in a church group -- can't remember the name of the group. Daddy and the group hollered and shouted when they performed at church, thanking God and giving praise. But were they really committed to the Lord's works? After church, the group stepped in the back, pulled out their liquor bottles and drank. This was ridiculous. Couldn't these dummies at least wait until they went home to enjoy their guilty pleasure? In the back of the church, you could hear them cursing and using vulgar language. One would say, "Give me that damn drink," then an argument would ensue with someone passing licks, usually it was my daddy. This was after they had just left church and sung. What losers! Oh, you couldn't tell my daddy anything. He was such a hypocrite, poor thing. Why did they have to get drunk and try to perform? They sounded horrible, but they thought they sounded good. After all, they were in the Lord's house. Couldn't they at least show some respect?

Another Drunk Episode

Just around 10 o'clock one night, there was a knock on the door. Momma opened the door to find my daddy drunk and disoriented. He said, "Lady, can you please direct me to my house?" All the children laughed and shouted out loud, "Daddy you are home. Hah! Ha! Hah! Ha! We laughed until we couldn't laugh anymore, but the smell of the wine, liquor or whatever caused the pungent scent on him destroyed my appetite. Well, after that, our daddy acted well for a while. Months passed, and then when we thought things were getting better, a friend discovered my father on the railroad tracks late one night. First, Lard thought Daddy was dead after nudging him for a while. The little small framed man sighed. He said my daddy looked like a toothpick lying on the rails. Lifting him, Lard managed to get him home. What a loser. If the train had come, this little man would have been dust along the railroad. It's stupid for someone to drink until they lose control of their senses, vomiting, limping or even passing out. What stupidity? The train could have killed Ed. Ha! Ha! Let me think, would this have been a blessing or a curse …? In my mind, it might have been a blessing because, finally, this evil man would be gone. No more running, no more crying and no more hiding! In spite of me saying this, I loved my daddy, but his actions caused me to have these negative feelings about him.

Mother's Illness

My mother's brain seemed to dysfunction every three years. This was a pattern because of my father's abusive behaviors causing her to snap. One day, my mother tried to emerge my younger brother in water, baptism, she thought. Eva, nearby, pulled my little brother out of the tub. This time my momma stayed in the facility about three months.

Here we go again, back to the monster's place--my aunt's home. After my mother had gotten better, she was reunited with her family, and we celebrated her homecoming for a while. Our father, an alcoholic, resumed his torture, verbally and physically. Every weekend the family ran to escape his explosive temper. I escaped through dreams, projecting my thoughts into a world filled with pleasure. There in my dreams, my family was made up of love. Love was spurring from top to bottom. My, what a delight! Here is another one of my poems, which I wrote to express my thoughts.

My Mother

Defeated by my heart what can I do?
Not showing my feeling for lack of rejection
never allowing my mind to roam or grow
because the sins of my mother, don't you know.
I hid in shame deep down in my soul
always focused, my mental state low. Afraid to
be a child, but too young to be an adult,
Confused, misused, but never giving up.
If I could only relax and be a child for just
one day, giggle, laugh and even play.
But my mother's illness got worse, so hey, it was
my time to be a parent for just another day. It
was hard being a parent, yet still a tiny child just
living on instinct struggling to
Survive. Although confused and in mental pain,
she was my Dear Mother, sweet, sensitive and
a joy to my name.

Chapter 6

Racism and an Abusive Father

When I got older, I experienced the worse kind of racism: our crew was working on a tobacco machine, putting in tobacco, as it was called, when a couple of workers asked to use the bathroom. This was something simple, I thought. The boss lady grimaced at us with such hatred, it scared the mess out of me. Then she said, "We don't allow niggers in our home." Shocked! Why were blacks treated inhumanly? This was absurd. Color shouldn't have been a factor, because God is love, but I remained silent. It was just not normal, I thought secretly. The boss lady even gave John, Mary and the rest of the crew, one jar to drink out of. What was she thinking about? We didn't want to drink behind someone else.

Same scenario. Working with a different boss, we got the same reaction. After working for hours, Dana and I decided to walk from the field to use the boss bathroom. We forgot about the prior incident after all, we were teen-agers. We walked from the field and ask the nice boss lady to use the bathroom. Oh, you would think we had committed a murder. Do you know that smile changed into a frown and that mean big fat white lady almost frighten me with an expression on her face that made me want to run. Ya'll are niggers, we don't allow niggers the use of our bathroom, are you crazy? Get your black ass out of my sight.

Why did this woman call us niggers anyway? Did she think all blacks were niggers? Nevertheless, we kept working, even though in the back of my mind, I wondered why so much hatred targeted the colored people, a slang whites used so readily. Why is the color of my skin considered a banner of shame? Yes, it hurts. The hurt goes deep down to my soul. There were so many times when racism was bluntly displayed in my face, but this one time Dana and I were going to my aunt's house to visit. It seemed that what happened took stupidity and racism to another level. Dana and I had walked for miles, on our route to visit Aunt Lay. The road was endless, and then out of nowhere a carload of white teenagers stopped. They asked, "Niggers do y'all want a ride?" We both said, "Yes," then they said this, "We don't ride niggers." Why did we say yes anyway? But back then, we didn't know any better; we were just kids. They could have been serial killers or something. The white teenagers sped off but later returned and asked us again; this time, we declined the ride. God truly protected us that day.

Back to the Field to Work

It was summertime and time to go to work. Man! And another year of hard work in the blazing sun! Nothing to show for our efforts! Eva, Dana and I had only had a couple of outfits for the whole summer. This was the same routine every year. Boy, I wish things were a wee bit different. We worked so hard. We went back to school blacker, even darker, than the year before. Black. Sure it might have been okay for the people wanting a tan, but we already had one. I'm saying it because at the time, people seemed to think light skin was in. Although one of my sisters was brown skinned, even she was blue black after the summer's heat started beating down on her little frame. When the summer was over, Mr. Ed brought us one dress for school and one pair of shoes. We were very appreciative though. Other students came back with several outfits. Our classmates who also proudly showed off their new clothes paraded fancy dresses, jewelry, shoes and other accessories.

Why Is the Color of My Skin Considered a Banner of Shame?

Why is the color of my skin considered a banner of shame?
Why is every walk I take limited to my name?
Why do they wonder, if I'm not there?
Without any doubt, do they really care?
My black skin isn't a razor blade
It's soft, COME closer, you will see
It's soft and spongy the same as thee
Extra burdens are placed on my back every time I go out my front door.
But hey, the power of love is strong, so I continue to march on to face the uncertainty of this day with a smile because I believe, I believe

With a passion, the power of love will conquer time and return it to its rightfully home
We won't be measured by our color; or judge for our state of being. It's a scope of thought because we all will be kin. It will be part of our language
Part of our flesh, then the widow tree will bend, unleashing the spoils of time.
That has crippled men from the beginning of time.

Signs of Della Relapsing, Poems and More Drama and Infidelity

There were always signs when Mother's nerves were acting up, like when she stayed up all night long, and there were pots and pans banging throughout the house. Della was up when I got up to go to the toilet no matter what time it was. And another telltale sign was her appearance: all of a suddenly, Mother didn't care what she looked like. Here hair that was usually pressed well, now was standing up on top her head. Even Della's voice sounded strange, and her behavior . . . well, it seemed that she was playing a game, a game that only she understood. Eva, Dana and I didn't know how to handle this situation. What would you have done! Was she relapsing again? I pondered secretly. Momma's illness got worse; she started back talking to herself and acting strangely.

Just out of the blue, on a warm summer day, I saw my momma and daddy near the ditch by our house. Both of them were kneeling by the edge of the ditch. What was going on, I thought? Moving closer, I heard her tell him to bow down; he did. His knees were shaking like a bowl of jelly. Secretly, I was elated. Ha, Ha! This man was finally afraid. Why? When Mother, Della, was sick, she had the strength of a raging bull. She threw Daddy around like he was a ball. Now, getting back to Momma and Daddy staring up at the sun: Momma ordered Daddy to "Look up at God." After several hours, Momma stepped in the house. It was in the nick of time because my little sister, Lora, was about to drink some bleach. My mother grabbed the bottle from her in the nick of time. Then one day, several neighbors came to see what was going on with my mother. Della met them at the end of the porch and before their feet touched the top step, Momma threw ashes at their feet. In a panicked state, they proceeded to run like hell. All the kids laughed! The neighbors ran like wild bears and tigers were after their behinds. Oh well, what did you expect, she was mentally ill.

Reflecting . . . when I was in the third grade, my mother was again committed to a mental illness institution. A child came up to me one day and said, "You all must be some bad kids because you caused your mother to go crazy." Those words shattered my life; my heart was so heavy, and I never forgot those words. That's why the word "crazy" . . . well, it makes me sick. I loathe this word. Why did people always call my mother crazy? The next poem is a special honor for all the mothers. I initially wrote it for a friend because her mother had surgery to amputate one of her legs.

A Trumpet to My Dear Mother

Cultivated by love
Savored with honey and spice
Topped with morsel with a delicacy of honey
plums and rice
Her smile is topped with raisin as her eyes glitter
as they shine
She is very humble and meek because she reflects
what is nice.
Her strengths have uplifted our family through
the peak of disasters,
rising high as an eagle to fly as the wind breezes
by
With her guidance our family have prospered and
moved forward in life
She has guided us through endless struggles,
remaining true to her belief
By giving God the special honor the keeper of
the gate.
She is a scented flower, sprinkled with cinnamon
and spice, she has all the
special ingredients because that's our mother and
she is truly nice.
All the life lessons we have learned, she has been
instrumental in giving
us the tools for success. She has helped provide a
haven, a place
where we all could rest. She is the rock of our
family.
The rock that have laid down the foundation

to build and govern our lives, she has all the special qualities,
she is humble, caring, honest devoted and so full of life.
Thank God, for our mother, she is the glue to our success,
she keeps our family motivated to love each other unconditionally
applying grace because, we all, eventually will be put to a test,
a test to hinder our faith. She is our cohort and such a devoted friend
She is the person God has chosen to provide encouragement to uphold
what is right. Her love is endless and relentless; providing tireless hours because
She secretly knows that God
Is the Keeper of the Gate.

Mother's Best Friend and the Woman Who Stayed with Us

There was one lady who was very supportive to my mother; her name was Nan. She saw past the mental chaos that my mother was experiencing. Mrs. Nan's meticulous character and friendly nature were very encouraging to my mother. She talked to my mother and always had words to lift my mother's spirit. This helped her more than I could've ever imagined, just knowing that someone cared was more therapeutic for my mother. When my mother was gone, my father, who was customarily abusive, magically became a good father. This is my opinion--totally mines. My siblings might recall things differently. He even brought home two women to help out with the chores since momma was resting in a facility. Wasn't it nice of him? He instructed us to call the women he brought home Aunt Sue and Aunt Sally. Mr. Ed, even let them sleep with him in Mother's bed. I guess it was all right; after all, Momma was gone. Both were older and more seasoned than my father, such nice women. Such a pity though, Momma wasn't there to enjoy the fun they had in her bed. The moaning and groaning they made at night did keep me up, but boy, it was exciting. But why were Aunt Sue and Aunt Sally both in bed with daddy naked? Why didn't Momma tell us about them? They never visited us when Momma was home. Daddy told all the kids that he brought them home to help him out, but Mother was gone. Did mom know about this?

This was dandy with me because they cooked good food but was he telling us a lie?

After needed therapy, mother returned from her most recent stay at the mental illness facility. Her skin was flawless, and she looked well rested. She had a womanly figure that was well proportioned, I guess that why daddy acted the fool. Mother was a beautiful woman, her brown skin and physique caused men to stare every place she went, but she acted like she didn't even see the men that were at her disposal, she loved Mr. Ed. I thought to myself, it's a pity she had to go away for awhile to get rest from her family. Nevertheless, our father pampered her for two to three months after she returned. After that, she was free target practice for his rages--back to the old drawing board, running, hollering etc.

There were so many times mother was committed just to rest, but at one time father let a close relative baby-sit all the kids. It was a male relative; after all, my father thought it was okay for him to baby-sit. What a fool. This relative offered Dana and me a drink. The drink looked funny; we asked what was in it, because it looked like gel mixed with a milk-like liquid. We didn't drink it.

Sadly, we found out later the relative had mixed the liquid with body fluid. He wanted us to drink his body fluid. Was this person insane?

But nevertheless, mother returned, happy and filled with hope; she had faith in her marriage, her children, and in God.

Shortly after our youngest sister, Lora, was born, our mother relapsed once again. This was a new chapter for Eva, Dana, Dora and me. All the older girls had to assume duties around the house and care for the younger siblings; we did the best to our abilities.

One day when I was grown, my younger sister, Dora told me my father called her names. What kind of names, I asked? She had a bad eye, and he called her taunt eye. Growing up, my sister was plagued with eye problems, so when he called her taunt-eye, it damaged her self-esteem. She expressed her low self-esteem by acting older and being fast. She was very easy, as they would call it.

Dana got married at age 16. She was more mature than my older sister and me. She was an old soul in a child body. Well, that was the way I felt personally. This girl had a way with older people; they would shower her with beautiful gifts and food. The rest of the kids would reap the benefits; for example, the delicious food that they gave her would, in turn, be given to us. The next poem reflects how a little girl suffers in silence.

The Little Lost Girl

The time is not known, the hours are not yet born
The someplace is hidden from a child cuddling a warm blanket
Why is the life of a child limited to one's imagination?
Then out of shame and fear, the little lost child speaks; she says this
I am only one but to a child of few I am a little lost girl
I am not defiant in the earlier stages of my life
Why are my instincts restricted to only my mother's face?
But I am but one, a child, little but lost
A child in quest for the embracement of her mother's arms
A child that will never see the wrinkles in her father face or hear
The loudness of his voice, but after all I am a little lost girl
I have no ponytails, only a single braid, silky black that rests down
My small narrow head
My sisters and brothers are asleep but thoughts of play
Are interrupted by the sound erupting from my mother's room.

I am quiet, as I escape to a pleasurable time,
where there is
no interruptions, no delays but where a little lost girl
Can go, can laugh and can be reborn,
Where a child has a momma, papa and siblings
and has the highest regards for life and love. As
she sits in the corner secretly, abruptly she falls
to asleep

Mother's Break Down

During the years, my mother had several nervous breakdowns, but she would bounce back, reuniting with her kids. We thought she was on vacation and needed rest from being Mr. Eddie slave. She was a devoted wife, even when my father continued to have affairs that agitated our family's life. It was a way of life: fighting, running around, drinking and altering all of his children's self-esteem. Still in the back of my mind, I wonder if people only knew how hurtful the name 'Crazy' was to me: it tortured me and hung over my head like a cloud. How could I tell the little girl in me it was my daddy causing all my mother's problems? He was the menace. Did Daddy care? Hell No!

      I'm angry now!

Chapter 7

Earlier Years of Bliss: Dating, new Relationships, marriage Boos Boos, and more

It was the late 60s, and it seemed to me that the world had become carefree; it was all about dancing, having friends over, and partying. "Let's Party" was our motto. We didn't realize we were poor; the 60s was the time to lose your mind in the music--no cares, only the sound of music. The Supremes, The Temptations, Smokey Robinson, The Beatles, Earth Wind and Fire, and whoever was on top at that moment, that's what really mattered to me. It was the decade for the hot pants and shorts; the shorter the pants, the more whispers we got from the boys.

We had house parties, Kool-Aid, popcorn and chips. All of this was a must back in this decade, people just enjoyed the simple and wholesome life. Life back then, welcomed the free spirited.

When I started dating it became confusing and rewarding, because now there was a man in my life and life became centered around our passion. Old saying goes, *friends first then lovers.*

Lard was huge, medium height and dark. With no warning, I fell in love, blinded by sheer passion. Come on, you know how it is when you're in love! Suddenly, everything about this guy was beautiful, even though, he was triple my size. What really made me interested in him was that Lard (that was his name) always bought me things, simple things like candy, soda and ice cream. Since I came from a large family, there was not too much of anything around our house, this really attracted me to him. Lard's family was small, with a total of four people in his family.

When Lard broke the cherry, my life changed. Back then, that was an old saying for your first sexual encounter. Now, sexual gratification was my passion because it became an everyday or night thing. Stimulated by my newfound passion, my sexual desires became a must-have; it was more than a passion it became my obsession. What had my black behind been missing? The thrill takes me back to the good ole days. When lying on the dirt was a sign of luxury, this guilty pleasure probably would be call cheap today.

Late one night, my lover and I were having a heated sexual encounter, when out of nowhere, out of the corner of my eye, there were lights, coming closer. "Stop fool, it's, Daddy!" Trying to get my pants from off the ground, I made it before he pulled up in the back yard. If my daddy had caught me, my butt would've been red for days. Daddy's car arrived, speeding into the driveway. Man, the fear in my heart! Suddenly out of nowhere, our dog snatched up and ran off with my shirt. It was horrible! But my bare chest made it before my daddy turned the path into the driveway of our house. Ain't that what counts? The taste of honey was truly amazing but costly. All my energy was devoted to reaching the ultimate sexual high. Weighing 100lbs <soaking wet, my butt was small compared to a heavy butt; I was teased daily; people called Lard fatso, but I knew what Lard had to bring to the table and the thrill was more than what people said. Lard, nevertheless, was my love; it crazy because he showered me with food first, this finally sealed the fate, I fell hard. Plus, the sex was amazing, this fat man knew what to do. What was supposed to be a long life with my boyfriend turned out to be only a young girl's infatuation? Lard was very considerate at first; all his attention was focused on me. Then the unthinkable happened: he started spending more time with his friends: Jimmy, Ray and David. Lard had lots of friends. That's why I didn't question why he wanted to hang with them more, clueless to the whole infidelity.

He went to a party one night, but there was a wild card-- my sister Dora was there, and she saw him with another girl. Lard had no idea Dora would be there. At the time I was mad with my sister, but she hinted around so I would find out about Lard cheating. I confronted him, but he claimed he was not at the party. Who do you think I believed? My sister, of course, she had no reason to lie. After that, he became a real ladies' man, but he was unbearably jealous of me. We dated very heavily until he graduated-- but did he really? I heard it through the grapevine that Lard needed more credits to graduate.

Getting Married

Before I graduated, I found out I was pregnant. Another boo-boo . . . I didn't have the tools to raise myself. As a result, I decided to move in with my sister because Mr. Ed was giving me Hell., she lived in Virginia. She told me, "Just because you are pregnant you don't have to get married." But I said, "I love him." So, we got married.

It was not even a month before things changed. Ouch! Forgot to tell you I moved back home with my parents. Lard's infatuation with me seemed to simmer away. There were unexplained arguments, then out of the blue, he would leave. Being married was hard, then the worse thing happened, we moved in with his mother. This was a mistake I regret up until this day; you think Mr. Ed was hell, this lady was his match from hell. Later we moved into our own house, because his mother was used to having her way; I kissed ass for breakfast supper and dinner.

Affairs

Finally, after months, we moved into a small apartment and waited for the arrival of the baby. Our relationship got so bad that we were fighting every chance we got. Lard was a cheater; his suspicious attitude caused me to suspect infidelity. I paid a neighborhood girl name Janet to find out some dirt on my husband. She, in turn, started having a relationship with him. Jan was sloppy looking, and her shape needed a makeover. She had more in the front than the back. This man was a piece of work. What do you think about that? This is what love is? I thought. One night I was looking out the window when I saw him being dropped off. Lard kissed the lady in the back seat and said bye as he closed the door. Arrrrrrrrr, there goes my temper. When he came in, I threw some hot water at him. He ran down the street and the chase continued. Even though I had a potbelly, man, I could run. I threw a butter knife at him; it made a dent on his rear end. Lard yelled, "Ouch!" Then he turned around and started chasing me. Domestic violence with a big Bang or was it? Finally, my little baby boy was born; he was born during a very breezy winter. He was a very chubby little baby.

The last straw was when Lard threw my clothes out in front of our apartment. A crowd of onlookers gathered. The people couldn't believe the lack of respect, this man had for me. One neighbor got so mad at my husband that he told him, "Man, you don't treat your wife that way, what is the matter with you!"

Even with the new baby, Lard continued his deceitfulness. At this point, we were fighting every day. It got so bad, I approached my mother. "Momma," I said, "Lard is treating me terrible; we are fighting every day." Momma Della smiled. She said, "Child, it is about time you woke up. That man ain't right. Sure! You can come back home. My daughter will not be a doormat for anyone." Even my daddy said, "Honey, you can come home; you are always welcome in our home." I left Lard shortly after this incident because his deceitfulness got worse. Ed, my father, had seen Lard on several occasions flirting with lots of women; Lard even missed work to be with those women; this cost him his job.

I spent about two months in my parents' home, then I left after a conversation my mother had with my uncle. Momma beseeched Uncle Jeff to let me stay with him and his family, that was the best thing that ever happened to me, a change of scenery was what I desperately needed.

Moving Away

It turned out that my mother's brother and his family took me in. The important thing about moving out was that I got to see how other people lived. My Uncle Jeff was totally different from my father: he cherished his children; his family didn't have to worry about little things, such as a shortage of clothes and a little food in the house--quite the opposite of when I was living at home. Uncle Jeff's family's closet was filled with name brand clothes and it seemed there were clothes for every occasions. They were truly blessed. That is when I truly learned that all fathers were not the same. It's amazing that there was life other than the controlled life we were living at home.

My uncle's wife, Aunt K, was a jewel; she treated me like her own child. She was light skinned with beautiful features and a heart of gold. Words can't express how I felt about her. These were exciting times, especially when Aunt K's mother came to visit. She was a stockily built woman; her husband was small and short. My Aunt K's mother would fuss about anything; she was really funny. She basically was a nagger.

Uncle Jeff's youngest daughter, Little K, was a busy body: She stayed into something. She was named after her mother but lack her mother good nature. Little K was bad; she would do things just to make her grandmother mad. "Josie did it," she would say, when she got caught doing something wrong. She was a little troublemaker. Aunt K helped me get a job at the plant where she worked; I was so happy because now, I could send money home to help support my baby boy, little Lard. My, it felt good being an independent woman. While living at my Uncle Jeff's house, every weekend, I still went home to visit my son who was living with my parents. My estranged husband and I kept in touch. Oh my, I still loved that fat man! What a pity! Then, like always, I decided to reconnect with my husband, Lard. I continued to work. This was my outlet. It gave me pride. The feelings I had about working were unbelievable.

After thinking about more opportunities, my parents moved to the big city of Raleigh. My father got a job working with my Uncle Jeff. Daddy finally was making a decent salary to support his kids, quite pleasing to my mother. Things now were falling into place, so I moved back in with my parents.

Things aren't always gonna be the way we want them

Chapter 8

Reuniting with My Husband, Dating, New Adventures with men and more Cheating

Reuniting with my husband, Lard, was another chapter in my life. It was hard to trust someone who had been unfaithful time after time. Lard and I lived with my parents for a while then we moved into our own place. I discovered that I was pregnant again. In due time, Lard got a job in the same city where we lived. Everything was normal for a little while; however, I'm saying it with reservations. Then one windy day, I caught him with a thirteen-year-old girl, named Tootsie, who lived next door. The girl was getting out of my husband's car before school let out. Having a woman's instinct, something told me to go to the bridge by my house. At the bridge, I waited because something about that day just wasn't right. Finally, my wait paid off. Lard dropped Tootsie off near the bridge. I ran and ran. Can you imagine a pregnant woman running around and about to go into labor at any time? It was hard, but I beat them home. Since Tootsie was my neighbor, it was easy to confront both of them together. They denied it, of course, which pissed me off. Enraged, I chased the thirteen-year-old around the car. About this time, my thirteen-old sister walked up. "GG, did Tootsie go to school," I asked? "No!" GG said. Now, the drama started again. More running and cursing. I did this until I got tired. A few months later Mack, my middle child was born. Lard continued to see the thirteen-year-old, unbeknownst to me.

We decided to separate. Shortly after, we reunited once again. He continued to cheat and stay out all night long. Let me tell you this: do you know this man even said he was locked up in the movie theater and that's why he didn't come home one night. He expected me to believe that foolishness. Ha, Ha!

Lard . . . well, this man had lots of buddies, one in particular, Melvin always seemed to pay me a visit when Lard was gone. It seemed Melvin had a huge crush on me. How did I know? It showed in his demeanor, the way his eyes seemed to capture every inch of my body with a weird look on his face. "Melvin, you can't come in, I told you Lard is gone," I would say to him. Then one day, Lard moved me from the bug-infested house that we lived in. The house that we moved to was smaller, but at least there were no bugs. The bugs were so big in our previous house that they marched to the beat of their own drum, especially at night. They took over the house--it was saturated with bugs because the more I killed, it seemed there were more waiting in line. The man who owned this house didn't do proper repairs because the house was a shack. What do you think about that?

My Husband Cheating

A couple of months passed, and the same scenario happened again--his cheating. Again, after he was gone for several days, I spoke to my friend Daniel about my situation; talking to someone helped me put things together. Daniel, oh boy, he was built like a body builder. Women were drawn to him because of his physique. There were several women who actually hated me because Daniel liked me. Tired of my husband bullshit, I decided to go out with Daniel as a friend; when we returned, my husband was home. He saw me get out of Daniel's car. From that point, he interrogated me for an hour before slapping the shit out of me. "Lard why are you questioning me!" I asked. "You just got home from being with your outside interest." He was the unfaithful one, so why was I being punished? Lard proceeded to go outside. I thought he was going to confront Daniel, but he came back into the house. Was he afraid? After all, Daniel was built like a bodybuilder with fists that could knock out the average prizefighter. Lard walked in that door and beat the S*** out of me. My children were yelling and crying. Wow!

Do you know what happened next? He lost his job because he had stayed out a week and didn't call in. All of this was behind a woman. Stupid man, didn't you know you had kids and a wife to feed? I knew all about her –Ms. G., my husband's mistress--because she called weekly and gossip was flying high. Losing his job, my husband had no income, so he left to get another job out of state. I was pregnant for the last time, but I was unaware of my pregnancy. One of my neighbors told me about a job opportunity; the position was for a waitress. How exciting! Now there will be some money coming in, since my husband wasn't trying to support his kids. To me it was a lifeline, getting to meet different people. Also, the tips were good. I liked my job. My boss loved me to death. Every day at work I would go in the freezer where I pigged out on whip-cream, strawberries and other delights. Most of the time when I was servicing someone I had a mouthful of delights stuffed in my mouth. The customers loved my uplifting personality but some of my co-workers were jealous because people that gave me tips never gave them any. One lady had the nerve to ask, "Josie why people like you?" If you don't know how to meet and greet people with a friendly attitude, what you think will be the outcome? But one day my skills were tested, one man came into the restaurant with his white lady friend and as I was taking down his order, he asked me, why are you having baby? Wow, was this his business? Right there, I fussed him out but when I went back to dig more into his comments, he was gone. Thank you, Jesus, because my rant was about to be on. Don't try to humiliate me with a white woman; are you crazy fool?

During this time my husband and I were living separate, but still communicating regularly. I told my husband when I get too far along in my pregnancy that I would need him to be a standup guy for the children's sake. He said he would. Then, a sad thing happened. I stopped hearing from him; Lard even stopped coming home. What about his two boys? Did he care? I was too far now with my pregnancy. Needed some help, rent was due. Finally, I started dating. I also contacted the Social Services for help. At first, they gave me a hard time. I cried after talking to one lady named Ms. Thong. Feeling so small, she made me feel so worthless. I was so stressed out. I had no money and no food. How was I going to feed my two boys? Spirit renewed, I went back to Social Services and spoke to another person. Ms. Carr was nice, the opposite of Ms. Thong. She consoled me and told me that it wasn't her place to demean me, but to help me learn my options. After that, I didn't have any more problems with that hateful lady at Social Services about getting help.

A New Man in My Life

I continued to date one man in particular, Dario, before the baby arrived. Dario was a hulk, oh my God, um, um… His eyes were mesmerizing. After my third child, I said to myself, never will I go back to my husband Lard; he failed me three times. "Three strikes and you are out." Oh, he wanted to come back, but this was my final straw. Children do not ask to be born, so if you are not going to provide the care for them, you need to rethink being parents. It was time to move on. I was at the point of closing another chapter in my life by not taking my husband back, and life seemed more beautiful.

Oh my, there were men everywhere. My appetite for sex had increased and I dated one man after another. To me, sex was better when there was an element of getting caught. Anyplace was fair gain for sex. When one didn't act right, I moved on without pity or compassion for them. I continued to date Dario before I had my little girl.

One day I asked Dario to buy me some pampers for my newborn baby. "No!" he said. "It's not my child." If you could've seen my black face, you would have seen rage written all over it! As I looked at this guy who weighed 200lbs or more, I said, "You knew damn well I had children before we dated, so if you will not buy me pampers, you need to get the hell out of my sight. I don't need a person that can't help me out." He went and told my mother. Even my mother asked me about it. "Momma, he got to go," I said. But later, he brought pampers for my baby. Now what do you think of that? I dated this young man for a while afterwards.

One day, my sister told me she saw Dario with someone else. I asked him about it and he said it wasn't him. Again, whom do you think I believed? My sister, of course, who has nothing to gain from this man? Needless to say, I told him Meatie had no reason to lie. While I was still seeing Dario, I decided to make breakfast for him. I'm going to surprise him, I thought. I cooked grits and eggs. It turned into a disaster: the grits were horrible. They tasted bad, man; they tasted like wood. To tell you the truth, I wasn't good at making breakfast. We continued to date for years. Then one night, after a night of heated passion, Dario told me he was getting married. At first, I thought he was joking until he repeated it casually. "What! What did you say?" as I sat up in the bed. "Are you serious?" He said, "Yes." "Get out!" I yelled. It was stupid what came out of his mouth. Dario said, "Josie, I can help you more when I get married." Rage... hate... What the hell was this man talking about? Did he take me for a fool? Well, now, he gonna see the real Josie, the one I covered up to appease his needs. Cursing up a storm, I called Dario every name under the sun, black b**** and f*** until my mouth became dry. The next thing that came out of Dario's mouth was alarming, "When you get older and your looks fade, you're gonna wish you kept me," Dario said. Well, no, he didn't go that route. My counter attack was, "I'm not old and until that day comes, you can get the hell out of my house," saying it with a force that surprised me. Sadly, he didn't think I wasn't good enough but for one thing, Sex!

Regretting the Time

Raising my children with no help from their dad was hard; it was a challenge every day. Basically, I matured along with my children. I didn't know the gravity of being a parent. I heard people say, "Look at that lady, she left her children home alone," or the person "should have known better." But, when you are younger, the severity of certain things doesn't register. Even though a person might be grown, sometimes their brain has not caught up with their mind. Some of my actions were not great, because of my high sex drive. That's why today, when I see younger people making the kinds of mistakes I made, I'm sympathetic.

Now, dating was another cup of tea. I dated my share of men, but never allowed my children to call them, Daddy. My kid's father helped raise other people's kids while his own went lacking. We lived at the Salvation Army because I couldn't afford to buy my kids new clothes and other necessities. Haven't you ever heard people say, "Child, there were times in my life when I had to steal and do this and that to survive. It's a cope out. The time it takes doing something wrong, we could be doing something positive. For me, God intervened a lot of times because there was no way I could have made it without His contributions in my life: He helped me through durable times. There were times when my children were small, begging for help wasn't an option. Bills were overdue and rent eviction notices were on my door, I had to swallow my pride and go to the Salvation Army, because my children were my priority, not my pride. Somehow, I managed to pay the bills. When I went for help for my bills, there were many who talked down to me, but my focus kept me strong. So many nights I cried. At such points in your life, your pride is so low and your spirit is broken, but it's only a survivor's skill that keeps you going. As I endured hardship and faced nights without lights, I swallowed my pride and solicited more strength.

A mother goes above and beyond a mile to feed her children. God gave me the strength to face another day with aspirations of hope. In my quest for closure after years dedicated to self-gratification, my thoughts drifted to the Bible.

No Time to Pray

It is morning, as I wake up from my sleep
I don't say a word of praise.
I don't ask God how I thank him for all
his amazing grace.
I don't thank God for just simply being alive.
I don't thank God for the tragedies I endured
while raising my children alone.
I know I shouldn't just approach God only when I
am in need. I got to break this cycle and give God
the honor, the supreme of all things. I know I should count
My blessings since my life is at ease. I just got caught up with forgetting, because only God knows our
needs. It doesn't take a fool to know how God really cares. If I can get up and eat every day, why Not at least show him that his holy grace is

shared.

His love is universal; God is waiting for your call. It is up to me now not the next person in line.

Let's change the subject back to my dating. I rekindled my relations with a past lover. Then another former lover returned, Dario. Speaking casually, I told Dario I had a new friend. Not taking no for an answer, he gave me a passionate kiss. That made it too hard to reject his advances, but gathering my thoughts, I refused the call to the bedroom. After a brief visit, we walked to his truck. Inside was another matter: Dario continued to kiss me, leaving a kiss mark. Finally, Dario left but he continued to pay me a visit even though he stated he was married. But it was over sexually. During the next couple of years, I dated men left and right. It was like changing my shoes. If one didn't do, there was another. Since I was badly hurt by my husband, I didn't let another man get next to my heart. Being very sexual, it was a paradise for me to have so many men at my disposal.

One guy I dated was a psycho named, Tim. Tim drank for breakfast, lunch and dinner. When he drank, his eyes would revolve around in his head; it was weird. I dated him for a while because he helped me out a lot. His body was perfect which enticed me to him in the first place. However, his face needed a makeover. Tim and I fought almost every day, usually over sex. Sex was a must for me, but he was addicted beyond my comprehension. Tim could never get enough which was odd to me, since I was usually the one who felt that way. Our life became so filled of destructive behavior; it was time to end the relationship. All my sexual secrets, Tim spread throughout the neighborhood. What a jerk, I thought. He tried to discredit me to all who would listen to him. Next door, my neighbor listened and sided with Tim. If Tim wasn't so good in bed, I would have been moved on, but that guy knew how to use his package. OH, he was skilled, oh my ass get hot thinking about it. But it was time for me to move on. I rekindled my relationship with a past lover, but it died out because he was seeing someone else. It was hurtful because I really wanted him back, but I didn't want to share his affections with another woman. The highlight of this relationship was that Dave lived at liquor houses like my father. He just liked going! Never did he want to go to the movies; plus, he complained about not having any money, but he could set up the entire liquor house. Ain't that odd!

Another man, more drama

I guess you could say my new boyfriend drank for breakfast, lunch, dinner and supper. Our relationship started off fine but ended up abusive on both parts. In other words, we fought like cats and dogs. We broke up every week; we got back together and fought some more. It was something about Curtis that captured my attention. Both of us were married but separated when we met. He continued through the course of our relationship to go back to his wife. It was a crazy period in my life; finally, I found someone I loved, and he was in love with someone who used to knock the socks off his feet. When Curtis's wife got tired of him, she would come up with ways to get rid of him after bleeding him dry. It was painful to watch. The sad thing about it was that everyone had told me step by step what would happen before it happened. When Curtis couldn't take any more of Cara's dishonesty, he packed up his bags and moved out. Curtis allowed Cara to control him for years, going back and forward, like a clock. When I came into Curtis's life, it was something that neither one of us saw coming. Both of us felt something that we just couldn't explain. We dated off and on for twenty years. Sadly, I had to threaten to leave Curtis and end the relationship with him to get him to marry me. Fighting and making up were the main ingredients of our life but passion made me stay.

My Children

I have three children, two boys and one girl. One of my boys, Mark, the youngest, was very mischievous when he was younger. He had a problem with stealing; you name it, he did it. One day I asked him "Why Mark, did you stop stealing, was it from the discipline?" He smiled and said, "No, Mom. I just got tired of stealing." Mark stole candy and went to school and sold it for a profit. He was an entrepreneur at an early age. Jr. was the perfect little boy; he was chubby with the prettiest smile. He was a mother's dream when he was young. Jr. rarely did anything wrong. My daughter, Kara, was one of a kind. She couldn't be left alone with other kids; she would fight and pinch them until they bled. "Kara, what have you done this time? I would ask her. "Nothing," Momma, she would say. Boot, one of my friends, would say, "I hope Josie isn't bringing that monster to my house."

Chapter 9

My Father's Accident Lies and my Parents Aging Process

Guess what? Even today, in the times we are living in, my father couldn't keep his hands-off women. He still tries his best to brush up against them when someone gives him a hug. This man would actually feel their breasts on a sly.

Then, one day my father had a liquor attack. He was yelling, stating he wanted to kill himself; they put him in a treatment facility. He was saying, "Hey, Aaaaagh!" Stupid, I would say. He had gone to the hospital because his nose would not stop bleeding. Walking in my father hospital room, I found him dressed only in his underwear. It shocked me, because his legs looked like toothpicks and his underwear was wrapped around his emaciated frame. Boy, he was bony! This sadden me, even though, my father had been abusive, this man was my father and I loved him.

But he was a trip, I remembered him taking me to different liquor houses while he drank and drank; while there, he touched every woman in sight, some of the women had no teeth, no hair and some were big, but this man didn't care; a woman was a woman to him. Some of the women he had affairs with, on several occasion, he got the bad disease. He liked all women, big, fat, and little--he had no preference. He liked them all. Some of the women drink like a sailor but pop didn't mine, he was looking at the bigger picture. Daddy hugged them as if they were a cream donut, kissing and licking all over their faces. Most of the women enjoyed this, they giggled like they were teenagers soaking in the attention.

One time, I went to court with him after he had an accident in the woods with a lady.
In court, on the witness stand, he told the judge the policeman was speeding, and he had to confront him. My daddy told the officer, "Man you need to slow down, "and the policeman said, "Can't this ride go?" The judge and the
people in the audience all laughed. My father later told the judge he was out courting and got stuck in the woods with his 400lb woman friend. The judge told my father to be careful next time; the people in court laughed and laughed. My father was found not guilty. He advised me not to tell my mother and I said you can count on me daddy. He gave me a couple of dollars, but as soon as I got home, I told her. This secret had to be exposed. Over the years, my father had taken the majority of his family members to liquor houses. It was a learning process for all the members in his family. It taught me to stay clear of drinking because some of the people at the liquor houses were very disgusting, why would anyone get so drunk that they can't walk or talk? It was crazy to me. Plus, my father's breath smelled like BM. But he graced every liquor house within a mile or two-mile range. Such a decent man, a man with morals, I would say. There were several times

when the policeman stopped Mr. Ed for drinking and driving. But this one particular time, he had a single car accident. The policeman stopped him and asked him for his license. "My father said, "Man, I drank my license up." Here we go again back to jail. The police laughed and laughed. The stupid man had trashed his car and it was totaled.

My Parents and the Aging Process

It is hard to see your parents go downhill, but the aging process is hard on a family that was once active. This process can be detrimental, since aging causes adverse effects on everything. Momma and Dad seemed to be losing control of the knowledge and wisdom they once had. Now, the children were the ones making all the critical decisions for them, very odd but a necessity. Recalling a time my mother wanted to purchase a vacuum, I told her it was too high. She purchased it anyway—a bad, bad decision. The vacuum was $1600.00. After receiving the vacuum and getting the bill, she hit the roof. The bill was outrageous. Della called the place to pick up the vacuum. They finally came but she still received notices. Now, it was time for me to write a letter to the company. Sadly, I had to literally threaten the people and insist that she had the right to return the vacuum within a reasonable time frame if she didn't like it. I also stated that my parents' rights would be honored in the court system if the notices continued. They backed away.

Then one day the unthinkable happened. My baby brother, Matthew died. He had a massive heart attack at work. He was only 34 years old. The pain ripped through me like a sword. It seemed my heart had been ripped out of my body that day; my heart stopped beating. The pain was unbelievable, in one second, I experienced all the stages of grief; denial, anger, bargaining but still haven't gotten to the acceptance yet. There have been many deaths in my family, but none of them hit me this hard. This one just felt like it ripped my heart out of its socket. Little Bro, as we called him, had a real soothing and calming voice. He brought love and laughter to all those around him. People used to say that he was an angel in disguise. He sure was that. I never saw this man get mad, which was very unusual. One of the most hurtful things about my brother's death was the lack of respect people had for my family. People should realize that even though their spiritual needs may be different from their family members, the innate love for their mother, father, sisters, brothers, aunts, and uncles are all glued to them throughout life. Although death happens, I still can't grasp its effects.

Chapter 10

Abuser Returned

Carl, a long lost relative, came back into my life. He was one of my abusers when I was younger. For some reason, I thought that since we were older, the desires he had when he was younger were just a mistake. I remember that I was so naïve. He asked me to take him to another relative's house. Something in the back of my mind kept nagging me for some reason, so I asked another relative to ride with me. It turned out to be the best decision I ever made. This person was a very close relative, needless to say. As I was driving, my relative that had abused me sexually as a child, proceeded to try to feel all over me; I was horrified. I kept telling him to stop, along with the other relative in the back seat. Totally shocked, I kept his hands off me. I pleaded along with my other relative for him to stop. After a long drive, we reached our destination. When we approached the house, the abuser asked, "Are you coming in with me?" I said, "We will be in later." As soon as he got in the house, I started my car and sped off, leaving him. He ran to the door but we both were gone. He later told someone it was dirty that I left him stranded. I cannot understand how a person gets sexual gratification from a close relative; it is unthinkable to me.

When Family Turns on Family

I had cousins who used to visit; but, somehow, we had a misunderstanding one day. Two of my cousins and their friend, paid me a visit. Instead of a friendly visit, it turned ugly mighty fast. One of my cousins stationed herself by the door and said, "Since you let us in, the police ain't going to do anything." I had to fight or flee. I fought. I threw one fat woman on the floor, but my two cousins then tried to double-team me. I had to leave my own house and run like hell to my neighbor's house. When I got inside the neighbor's house, my cousins still tried to fight me, but my neighbor said, "You are not going to double team her. One can fight her at a time but not two." We went outside and battled it out. I had one down again when I heard her sister saying, "Look at your face, she has messed up your face." Then one tried to hit me, but my neighbor would not let them double-team me. The sad thing about the misunderstanding was that it was over me not letting my cousin see her boyfriend over at my house. I had let my cousin and her boyfriend meet at my house for a while, but later told her if he thought anything of her, he would meet her at her home. In due time, we started back socializing; after all, blood is thicker than water. Sometimes in life a person needs to think about their choices and ask some serious questions: Why did you choose a particular kind of person? Are you choosing someone because of your father?

Getting Married Second Time Around

So, we decided to do the do. Both Curtis and I went to get the necessary papers in order to get married. If you could have seen our facial expressions, you would have noticed we did not look happy. We acted like we wanted to kill each other. The lady looked as if she was saying to herself, these two needed a mediator. As soon as we left the building, we got in a heated argument. K I hate you, you ain't nothing but a wine O, well, why do you want to marry me? He yelled back. As the argument became more heated, I drove about a hundred miles out of the way because we were fussing so hard I missed my turn. Rick tried to intercede in the argument.

The next day, it was time for the Big Event-- the marriage was to take place at a beautiful lake. There was a beautiful waterfall and ducks surrounding the lake . . . it was the most picturesque scenery that you ever could imagine. There was a smile planted so far on my face that even the President of the United States couldn't erase it. To my delight, my fiancé showed up after the fight the day before. Boy, was I relieved. The wedding was beautiful-- the groom looked like a million dollars, and the bridesmaids looked enchanting. Both my sons gave me away. I was happy; this was the day I had dreamed of for so long. After getting my dream man, things started to happen. Now, after getting my man, I had to fight to keep him. So, ladies, the struggle had only just begun. There is an old saying, "Be careful what you wish for." Like any marriage, there are good times, but there are bad times as well. But wait, why are there so many bad times? Did I make a mistake? I pondered this over and over again. Curtis seemed so preoccupied now that we are married. What was going on? Is there another woman? Well, those questions were answered. Unbeknownst to me, Mr. Curtis was continuing his fling and it was about to get nasty! Not again. Not another marriage gone wrong! More cursing, more yelling and riding to catch my man in the act, what had I gotten myself into? What was wrong with me?

Well, finally, my riding paid off, yes, I caught my husband over his girlfriend house. Would you believe this fool came out of the house with no shirt on, looking like he had swallowed a cat? Oh, you think I'm a fool now. There could have been another love triangle tragedy, but I just speeded off, crying and thinking about another marriage gone wrong. Curtis continued his journey to make my life miserable until I decided it was time to go. Let him have his woman, I'm not like my mother, forget this shit. Even though I loved him, he needed to know marriage is a lifetime commitment. Instead of telling Curtis I was leaving him, I told his friend, Rick. Rick told Curtis but instead of being happy, would you believe this man was highly upset. He didn't need me, he had his mistress and three was a crowd. Then something strange happened, Curtis started treating me with respect. Josie, please don't leave me, I really love you he said one day.

I submitted the following poem about marriage to my local paper.

When I Said I Do by JJB

When I said "I do I didn't know I would become
one instead of two
When I said "I do"
I didn't know there would be so many quiet
moments
Between us two, so many times I wanted to run
away, and say
"This is not in my script for today"
But pride, pride made me stay
But nevertheless, it was "for better or worse"
So I swallowed my pride and trudged (hiked) on
As I awaken from my sleep
Staring at my mate as he slept next to me, such a
temperate
(Calm) spirit
But God knew him first before me, he knew
That I loved him, and he loved me
A perfect timing for we
When I said, "I do,"
Our love was meant to last eternally, forever
through durable times
As I stand, looking into his eyes, I see grandeur
(splendor)
Beauty only God saw before he blessed me,

That beauty reflected a part of me
Now, we are one, he is me and I am he.

Ah, another chapter of my life is gone and passed. Secretly, I thought with every thought of pleasure, there is a thought of pain. It seemed like there was evil around every corner. Is there hope in my pursuit to search for happiness? Is happiness bounded and chained to a wall? I asked myself this and that. Has the past become so antique that we hunger for its existence? It's a shame that every year brings back more regrets instead of anticipations. Longing for a new adventure and a new purpose have always been my goals, but life has become a fight. Fighting to love hard has been a constant struggle on my behalf. With regrets, it is sad that we have to fight to protect our identities from others seeking to destroy. Why don't you take what you owe and leave mine alone! Why do I have to fight to get back what is mine? Why do I have to prove myself over and over again? I asked myself these questions over and over again. Smacking my lips, I struggled to uncover any idle thoughts and search for resolutions to this dilemma in my heart. Why are you broken when you get older? It seems that every bone ached. What do I have to look forward to? Then, it hit me: just being here is a blessing. People have become lost, gazing at the magnificent sky, walking on solid ground; we all should count our blessings. Think about the birds in the sky and how every winter they know where to go, Think about the squirrels and the other tiny creatures that survive the winter blizzard. Isn't it amazing? I found my purpose. It is never too late, speaking from a late flower. I want to devote my life to inspiring others to pursue their dreams. With every new chapter in my life, I will do my best to inspire others. Here are two motivational poems I wrote during my period of searching.

Success Means More than Riches or Fame by JJB

He is rich; he is poor.
How do you measure success?
Throwing titles here and there, does it really matter?
Sit down and think; do you feel a sense of relief?
Do the things you treasure dear give you an ounce of glee?
Does everyone around you secretly or honestly really care?
Everyone seems to think money is the key, but sit down and
Have a reality check.
Are the rich and famous happy, or are they always
In a state of beware?
Everyone gives you praise when you are up high,
But as soon as you fall, where are the people you once knew?
Stop! Look at the things in a different perspective. Success means more than money,

riches or fame. Life requires endless struggles, yet the pain is deep.
Being able to show beauty within, that's what makes a person unique.
Success isn't measured in monetary value because Valuables last only for a while. It is measured in the smiles of others,
As you approach them, now tell me, isn't it worthwhile? So when someone approaches you and asks you, what do you do? Just tell them you are a successful person because you have people who care and love you.

When I Close My Eyes

When I close my eyes, I see light. A light that shines through the spirit of destitute
When I close my eyes, I see challenges, challenges that I have yet to overcome.
When I close my eyes, I see honor. Honor that has long been comprised by the
Simple everyday person. When I close my eyes, I dream.
I dream of a milky white sky, filled with watermelons hanging on the rim of the
Stars, angled sideways, as the rainbow of colored birds, nest on the drops,
Flowing from the dew of the clouds. But suddenly, when I open my eyes, I see all
The blessing life has to offer. A new day, a new tomorrow, a new adventure waits.

It is a pleasure to be alive.

What is sane when you have all good intentions, but everything seems to fall behind the basket? There is no enjoyment anymore, only idle thoughts passing by. Still I have my dreams, my hopes as I face this world, a world that is plagued with violence, pain and death.

This passage is mainly for all the bullies, the people whose sole purpose in life is to pick on others. Remembering back, there were several women who talked about my mother and considered her mental state as a sign of weakness. Later in life, they, too, were plagued with some form of mental illness. My, isn't that odd. One lady, May, as we called her, approached my mother years later, stating she was sorry for talking about her problems because now she was going through similar scenarios. May had several breakdowns. Life has a way of correcting the wrongs done.

Sitting around thinking, I wondered what would have been my fate if my parents had been different. In other words, if there had been no abuse, no mental illness or whatever, would I have the same drive? Would I have empathy for others? Would I have been an inspiration to the silent ones whose voices are cold? Living is hard, but love is even harder. Just look around, today and tomorrow, we need love to assault the self-hatred in this world today. If we would only use our tongue to beautify the world instead of giggling and laughing about each other's imperfections, this world would thrive. You might say, I don't do that, but every time you pick at someone or make him or her feel small, you contribute to his or her downfall.

Angel in Waiting by JJB

Who was my brother?
Was he a man without flaws?
Was he selfish?
Was he a man that depended on others to plow the road for his success?
If I painted a picture of how he was, would you believe me?
But he was who he was, a man with character
A person with unbelievable wits
I remember his meekness, I remember, his smile
He had what you called the "it factor," whatever, he had it all
From a family brought up in poverty, to a child who surpassed in
His creativity in art.
Who was this person, we called brother, father, and son?
There are so many adjectives I could say
But he is gone now, so far away
He was born from the flesh of a woman
He was an angel in waiting because he touched
So many souls.
Why did he leave us?
My heart is heavy now; my tears are flowing, flowing

We will never forget your presence.
He was part of our heritage, a son, brother, father, uncle and friend.
He was an angel in waiting, for dust you have returned, until God says
wake up my dear son, your new life has begun.

I left out an important phase of my life, the years of being addicted to sex. It began when I had my daughter. My appetite for sex went through the roof. Since my husband (Lard) was gone, men in my life only fed my addiction for sex. There was a sense of hate for all the things I had endured. I treated men terrible. I guess it was my way of paying back Lard, but the men love the challenge.

In the 70s men were very abundant; it was like I was in a candy store, picking this one and that one. But most of the men were smaller than Lard, and boy they were good in bed. I was young, and it was my time; my husband had unleashed the beast, a raging bull ready to devour.

During my life journey, I met three friends, one was ten years older than me; another was a couple of years younger, and the last was a friend who was from New York. She was a trip. She was very petite but had the loudest mouth of the three and she knew how to party. The oldest friend out of the bunch, Fran, would go on vacation every weekend, stating it was her time away from her family. Another friend who was around my age, Jan . . . well, she had her share of problems. Every other weekend, Jan and Dave, her boyfriend, fought like cats and dogs. It was normal for her to sport a shiner. I asked her what happened? Jan stated she had walked into the door. Her eyes were bloodshot. Did she really think I'd believed that? Sadly, it was her boyfriend's fist. Dave looked blameless but packed a mean punch. I could not imagine someone doing that to me because the shit my mother endured from Mr. Ed, well, it would be consequences. Meg, my friend from New York, had her share of problems, also. Every other day, Meg and her boyfriend, Les, fought but Meg looked like the winner. Les's face would be so messed up: it looked like a lion or tiger had paid him a visit, scares were all over his face. My friend really scared his face. But the real fun began when we would get together and drink wine coolers. Fran, Jan and I acted like we didn't have a care in the world. No one was stressed out; as friends, we looked forward to the weekend, a time of relaxation and to drink wine cooler.

Meg had a bad temper, but this little petite woman was tough. I remember one incident in which an argument pursued with Meg and her boyfriend: Meg stormed into the Pizza Inn fussing and cursing. She got so loud that I thought we were going to get thrown out. Needless to say, I ended up taking her home. My boyfriend at the time, Dave, went home and boy I was furious with her. She messed up my actions that night because I was hot. We both were ready for some action because sex was the only thing that registered in my mind and made me forget, I was a single parent.

Rena was another friend, but she was very naive and let men use her. Her mother was really nice. One day I asked Rena to come go with me to visit Meg. Meg had moved across town.

When we arrived at Meg's house, she and her boyfriend were having a knock down drag out fight, but she had cooked some fish that looked mouthwatering. "Eat," Meg said, "because I don't have any appetite." Rena and I ate the delicious plate of fish, but they continued to fuss and a fight erupted. Not taking in the disturbances, my friend and I continued to eat the good food. Sure, two people were fighting around us, but the food was excellent, even though, fists were flying, we didn't help Meg.

Most of the times I visited Meg, or Ms. York, she and her boyfriend were fighting. Fussing and fighting were a part of Meg's life. She invited Rena and me over again because she was cooking a pig. "Yes, I'll be there with bells," I said. Another fight erupted. Man, the pig was still on the grill. Boy, Rena and I had another treat; we feasted off the food. When Ms. New York and her boyfriend fought, the food seemed to taste even better. It was selfish on our part for thinking such nonsense.

Back to my life . . . another boyfriend, more drama. All I could think of were my needs that prompted me to break up with my boyfriend. He never had money to give me, especially when I needed it for a bill. Oh well, it was time to move On because, a cheap man was not for me. At that point in my life, I couldn't imagine not having a man in my life. I didn't realize that I had a sex addiction until years later. While watching television one day, there was a discussion about sex addiction. It made me think, maybe, just maybe, that's my problem. I saw many people discussing their addiction to sex and the pain it had caused them. To me, sex was the best pleasure anyone could ever have.

Chapter 11

Whoa, My Family Is in Turmoil, Help, and Poems, Remembering my Sister, and a Trusting Spirit,

After my mother's surgery, the family struggled back and forth. Was this the best solution for my mother? When it comes to family, it is best to do things the democratic way. Every family member should have a voice, no matter how minuscule his or her input is; it's important. Also, confusion and tension are minimized if everyone has a voice; this is the democratic way?

The Unspeakable Illness by JJB
I speak, but no one hears me
I dressed as a flower, but no buds were found
Everybody scorns me
Everybody talks differently
Am I the only one who knows the secret code?
I'm a queen; I'm a dictator,
There is no other but me
Why don't they heed my call?
Don't sweet-talk me to appease me for the moment
I'm a person, but normal has taken a silent note
I'm not a nuisance, why won't you listen,
I know, I know
The flag of hope is soaring in the sky

Listen, people, Thoughts gobble up
My reasoning skills
In my hour of wisdom,
I'm unaided but alive

Inside my soul is dead, I cry! My pain is real!
Help! Help! I'm the unforgotten soul who society
has dispelled.

    This poem solely fits my sister; it all started when GG was in high school. Always reserved, GG took shyness to another level. Then after she graduated, she went to college. Shortly after going, we received a phone call stating she was in crisis due to her mental state. This is sad because we thought GG was finally breaking out of her shell. Daddy was very sympathetic to the needs of GG. I heard GG's breakdown was over a man; distorted from reality, this was a first look into a grave future for GG. All I know is that there had been a string of unforeseen events and predicaments due to GG not taking her medications. And she refused assistance of any kind. Let me fast forward. My sister GG has been off the chain this year and she refused to seek help. My parents' home had been the scene of unpredictable occurrences when Gag's mind led her to act in a disturbing way. She did anything from cleaning in her bathing suit in heels to cursing out everybody in her path. Usually, GG wore her hair sticking straight up on her head, thinking she'd created a new style. I'm not going to touch that. She suddenly became so controlling that she would stare at people when they visited my parents' home, expressing her input about germs and scrutinizing every move with retribution. If you couldn't take her criticism, well, it would be on. GG would curse and shout to get her point across. "Get out now," GG would say, if someone agitated her. My reply would be, "Girl, shut the f*** up." Who did she think she was? "You ain't my damn parent," I yelled back at her! Finally, one of my sisters had to take involuntary commitment papers out on GG.   When the policemen arrived . . .

Oh boy, it was a scene from a cop movie. She was kicking and yelling and acting up big time, saying she was going to f*** someone up. They finally had to restrain her. This slow progression of my sister's illness was sadly due to her feeling that she didn't need medication. She worked as a Personal Care Aide (PCA). This was her purpose in life; she thought. Whew! Our family has been down this road before and it's not a pretty ride.

First of all, getting help for your love ones is extremely impossible due to regulations. Sometimes HIPPA guidelines make it impossible for the family member to get a grip on the problem. Family members are subject to little or no information if the person does not want to disclose their personal information regarding their treatment plans. Even if they are clearly not aware of their mind-set, sometimes the family is treated badly. One example, our family experience was at a local hospital. One of the many times we tried to get GG help, we called the hospital after involuntary papers were taken out on her. The nurse working in the behavioral unit where GG was being treated stated that she doesn't "get in family business," after we inquired about GG's situation. She spoke sarcastically to several family members; it's a shame because this hospital has had numerous complaints in the past, being cited on numerous occasions, making their actions detestable. The hospital's staff members should have been more cordial. Are they professional people? No! They acted like people had to deal with their rudeness. If a person is clearly unsound, then I feel that they need supervision. It would save the family members undue heartache and distress if people would only listen. Society has blocked people from getting the help they need for the mentally disturbed. Regulations in place to protect the mentally disturbed have only made it difficult for family members to get the necessary help they need.

It happened to our family. Our family members wanted what was best for our sister; we didn't want to see her in any emotional distress. But our words went unheard. Please listen doctors, nurses and administrators and other professionals! The family members have insight about what is going on with their loved ones. GG lacked control, so she used her knowledge to try to control everyone else's situation. Why did my sister fail to realize that she needed medication for her mental state? It was a mystery to me. Can't let myself get all musky, and my thoughts switch back to more pleasurable times, we must understand that these are the lost ones; they need our support. They don't need to be tucked into a box and left alone to self- destruct! Oh, did I pray today? Please God, intervene to help my nephew. Allow him to overcome his troubles and his situation. This I pray! Please God, give my sister peace and allow her to deal with her mental state in a positive way instead of letting it control her in a negative way. In Jesus Christ I pray. Amen.

People say life is a learning process. So true. How can the rich get things they don't need-- credit, any place they want to live and other perks? It odd because, the poor needs perks not the rich.

Being an observer, I see things that are disturbing but there are limitations if you let life put a burden on you. It is especially hard if somebody knows that there is a mentally challenged person in your home. Even when you want to do something stupid, in the back of your mind, you question every action because you know you are constantly being judged. One false move and people will say, ain't that the crazy girl just like her siblings or parent? Thoughts drain my mind, and it is time to suck it up. People judge you differently when someone discovers that someone in your home has mental illness. You are frowned on and considered an outcast, especially if you are black because a lot of times this disease is frowned on in the Black community. Now, that's my personal take on it. Your circumstances might be different. To me though, whites are more prone to go to a psych doctor than a black person. Someone might ask, "Are you a nut case?" It's not me; it's my sister. What is this? It's sad!

Now, think about it: what would you do if you had a mother suffering from mental illness? How would you handle situations when people assume something has to be wrong with you also? Well, think about this, too: this illness causes people to suffer undo criticism and misery. Imagine several people in your family having this problem. Well, it seems the whole world thinks you are crazy. People with mental illnesses are judged every day. They don't need your pity, but understanding is the key. There are thousands, even millions, suffering from mental illness; some keep their illness hidden because it is still considered taboo. There is a wall facing you with a fence of protection as a guard. Even people you don't know seem to watch you like a hawk, or could it be your insecurities have caused you to doubt yourself? No encouragement is granted, only "I told you so," for any signs of weakness.   It's hard to face the future when helping others seems to be a burden. We all have good intentions, but here comes another burden disguised as a friend, a relative. There's trouble lurking everywhere.

I've always wondered why people seldom help others, now I know why. Some people seem to suck all the air out of their loved ones or their friends. That's what happened to my family. A family already in turmoil, with massive devastations, our family was heavily burdened down. There was back to back trouble. What was going on? Can we, as a family, discover our way back home? Then as soon as the fire was taken out of one thing, here walked in Mr. Trouble again. I called him Trouble because he seemed so innocent but wait and hear what I got to say! He came to visit all in smiles, but little did we know, he would cause so much confusion within one family. Days turned into weeks, until one day, someone asked Mr. Trouble when are you leaving? He replied, "I'm here to stay." No money was exchanged for his stay but only once, which shocked me beyond disbelief. He was cheap. How can you expect to live in someone else's home without asking? Then, my sister Lora told him he needed to pay my parents for staying in their home; he agreed, finally. Uncle J. paid toward the bill each month; he murmured, "Only a couple of bucks." Mr. Trouble only came out when it was time for supper. Within a couple of weeks, things turned in another direction. He stopped eating or socializing with the family, and then, all of a sudden, he became an introvert. He began to neglect his hygiene, which became intolerable because when a man smells, he stinks. Stopped bathing-- it was a mess, seemed he was afraid of water. This was just the beginning, the beginning of a nightmare: he became the ruler of my parents' home, causing anguish and discontent. We all thought he was trying to find his way. He started watching and seeing how things went on in the family. Little did we know he was taking it all in for his own purpose.

Then my mother had surgery and had to recoup in rehab. She finally came home but she was in a lot of pain. To make the matter worse, my sister GG returned. Along with Mr. Trouble, they ruled my parents' home. Mr. Trouble, my uncle, was telling people to leave as if this was his place.   "Get out," he told me one day. Wow! This man couldn't handle his own business. Then things got worse, he started drinking Vodka, it takes a man to drink Vodka. Vodka was too much for his fragile brain, that already couldn't connect the dots. Highly intellectual, Mr. Trouble couldn't comprehend he had a problem. His son had shipped him down South to get rid of him, because of his mental illness. Was it because he had had enough of his father's strange behavior? Ah, I wonder. The man acted well for a while, and then all hell broke loose. He ended up losing it again. Why did this man think he owned someone else's home? This man became Mr. Ed worse nightmare. He had taken over the headship of Mr. Ed's home. Topped with Vodka, that spelled disaster, Mr. Trouble was taking names and chasing people away.

All a sudden, Mr. Trouble started to sit at the table, drinking and checking out everyone who visited. Poor Dad, even though he was an alcoholic, it was still his house. We needed help to resolve this problem. We needed God's intervention for sure or was it a time to incorporate the ghetto way. There's a time in life when it's time to kick some butts.

Lonely Tourist by JJB

Where can I lie down and rest! My thoughts are weighing me down. I'm confused. I say this, I say that, why can't people understand that these are not my words? It's the words of a stranger, someone digging through the wasteland, to find gold. I'm a lonely tourist. I try to express my feelings but my words come out wrong. There are so many things I want to tell you but I'm like an infant, I just murmur, murmur because my words hold no key. Reaching out to gather my thoughts but I'm lost, I'm sinking! Where can I go for solace and serenity, searching through my chaotic state I asked! There are no holes to swallow my pain. I'm released back into society, only for just a short while; they hope I stumble before they take note that I'm a person lost. So, what do I do in the meanwhile? So, confused. There are several brick walls facing me, this I face every day.
How can I break through the chaos? Many people have failed, many have gone on but I'm the forgotten child, the ones you don't care to

mention or call. Living amongst the public, I pretend to be sane, shadows occupy my brain, and shadows occupy my will. I'm just fighting to get back what my dignity lost. Just a lonely tourist, mud in my eyes, sand in my shoes, is there a place where I can rest for a little while?

After exploring my dreams, I decided to reach out and help my nephew, Jamey. One man, so many thoughts. This is about a man struggling to reclaim his innocence, with negativity on one side and positivity on the other side; will he succeed or just become the man in the middle? He struggles. Will he overcome his troubles? It depends on him. This system is so corrupted. But the gift Jamey has, ah, it will bring tears to your eyes. Jamey's poems are masterpieces, some of the finest work of art. History will note him one day as one of the best poets of all time.

More reasons for writing this book

Truth…. There are so many reasons why my frustrations are being released in this book. It's a tool for others. For years, I struggled to keep people away. I was not affectionate because I feared it would come with a price. It took years to overcome this fear, the fear of letting someone love me and accept me without a price. Sometimes in life, a person has to reach and pull out everything they have inside to get to the next level. There are many waiting and hoping you will fail. It's just the world we are living in, so don't always take negativity personal. Just be the light that gives off inspiration within your heart, it will keep you safe. All the mayhems I've experienced have kept me strong. I'm surprised I'm still here. Thinking of so many incidents in my life, I focused on one that left me feeling abandoned. After helping a family member out, I was placed at the worse end of the stick. My kindness subjected me to undue criticism: "being nosy," someone said. But where was the family when this child needed them? My guard was exposed; it's hard for society to believe that family members are the ones doing the harm. Don't let anyone make you feel bad about helping someone in need because I did. Don't let it happen to you. Never let anyone doubt your sincerity, especially if it was done from "the bottom of your heart." Don't let someone deprive you of any acts of kindness. Have you ever wondered why few people get involved with other people's problems? Well, based on my personal experiences, when I did get involved to help someone, the system turned on me like a raging lion. No one wants to comprehend or believe that. Sometimes, families are the main ones hoping that you fail. Then people wonder when something happens, why so many people look the other way. It is because of bad experiences, not because they don't care--but society only welcomes a lie. Sadness, happiness, things go undone. Day by day, the pain hits home. Inside my home I grieved silently for my sister, for her failure to recognize her illness was real. Sadness embodied my spirit and I pondered the outcome of my sister's life. Suddenly, I thought of the times when GG laughed ... these were the memories that were dear to me. The veneer of my heart hurts. When someone in your family is in crisis, it affects all. My answer to you: please reach deep, bring out the warrior, and fight for your future—fight for your place in a world that only recognizes you as commodity. Say to yourself," I'm the one who will break this cycle." Don't let people poison your accomplishments. Be a fighter! Even in your sweet demure state, there is hope. Then, when life seems to pass you by, think of all the strength and progress you have accomplished. If you wait, dreams will be wasted on your pillow as you sleep.

Born from the womb of my mother, my sister's weakness was the cause of her downfall. So many times, I yelled out loud. If I let anyone in, I'll be called a coward, so I remain silent. Speaking about any problem isn't an option, so I asked, "Why? Lord, Why? Why does society embrace a lie when the truth has no meaning or reply?" Pained from history, hurdles and hills are placed at every corner. From the outside, a veneer of toughness and durability looked back from the mirror; inside my body is fragile and easily splintered. Secretly, thoughts swell; will there be a place of prominence in my future? I sit and ramble or go for a walk of pleasure to reaffirm my strength and belief in myself. "Life throws so many curve balls," but here is one story that affects us all. Thinking the justice system is half way fair, it took me for a ride. In this life, heated arguments can cause a loving family to become a time bomb. At this point in time, no one is immune from or can escape the raft of deceptions. Maintain the true self that is inside you; it will sustain you through the troubling times. Well! People say the world has changed and prejudice doesn't exist. It would be nice wouldn't it? Sadly, the ones that say it, more than likely don't live it every day. Maybe one-day people in this world should realize that color is just a word. Until then, child, "you better watch your back." There is an old saying, "Try walking in someone else's shoes." It would give you a picture of their life. Stop being so stereotypical; cast aside the older generation's attempts to negativity and strive to rise to another's cause.

Here is another curve ball: my nephew died after years of battling a debilitating illness. Poor fellow was all smiles; his spirit was unbelievable.

Little Stanley Man

To us he was a treasure
More than the eyes could behold
Little Stanley Man, my sister called him
He was treasured more than the finest gem or gold
To the spoken and unspoken words, he shared with us
It succored (relieved) our soul
It was the intangible (indefinable) things he shared with us
That descended deep down in our soul
Think about it, if Little Stanley Man could lift our spirit

Why can't we lift others as a token that we care?
Take the time and look around you, as he did so many times
The family and friends that visited him always remembered his breathtaking smile
Humble by all means. Is that so much to ask?
Now in the presence of Jehovah, God, let us pray
Jehovah shows each and every one of us the right path
When our fragile body leans another way
Give us the strength to plow on through the weeds that imperfect man
Put along the wayside on our journey to face another day
Help us to love each other unconditionally; that's the Christian way. Little Stanley Man has finally gone home. He is resting along with his cousin, little butterbean (Christian), Uncle Matthew and other beloved family and friends. Each of us has a chance to see Stanley Man, just be humble. Don't feed into this world with all its destruction, honor the highest of high. Give God the time he needs. I'm sure Little Stanley Man would say, "Come my family and friends, come and join the festivity." God will embrace you, I'm waiting. There is peace in God's arrangement because a tear will never grace my face again.

    Gloomy was the night when little Stanley died. Poor Stanley didn't have a chance; the world he knew was surrounded by aches, pain, surgeries, and discomfort. But, he brought so much joy to us. Stanley always embraced visitors with a smile. What can befall us, now? I say. Trouble? More trouble? When things seemed to be looking up, my sister lost her job.

This past couple of years has been a roll coaster ride. Wow, my nights have become so restless. Now, sometimes things happen for a reason. Don't get comfortable because a curve ball is just around the corner. This incident with my sister only made me more determined to succeed. But I learned a valuable lesson: the majority of the people are afraid. Being afraid is no option when your family member is in trouble. Search deep down; there is motivation, just reach for it.

Finding my voice, I approached people with a smile and handed out this letter. Will power? Oh no! It takes all the force inside. Stop abusing power! Corruption destroys everyone; we must stamp it out and correct it. Living in an unjust world, hardships are placed on our backs as we sleep. Sometimes, we see people being mistreated right in front of your eyes. It takes pride and fortitude to overcome. Where is the Black pride that the 60s represented? Where is the revolutionary fighter for justice? Why do we tolerate this behavior or treatment? What do we stand for now? We have indeed become silent, silent to the mockery. One of my favorite poets stated, "If we don't stand for something, we will fall for anything." We have become noiseless; our voices are only heard when we think no one is listening. Be a Man. Be a Woman; a silent man or woman is never heard. Say it out loud: "I'm afraid" and move forward. Don't judge someone because of his or her title; the facade can sometimes create a disguise, so make your judgments based on what is put forth. Gloomy, days are ahead, but where there is life, there is hope. Now, I'm highly pissed! Why do people always abuse their authority! This section is dedicated to the memory of my sister.

Remembering My Sister

Fired from her job as a detention officer, my sister was battling the fight of her life, breast cancer. She was fired because she wouldn't lie and say an inmate confessed to her. Two detectives that worked for the Rocky Mount Police Department interrogated her for hours. After she wouldn't say that an inmate confessed to her, they told her she could leave. Someone called her job; the detectives told her that if she didn't say what they wanted her to say, they would call her job. She was fired based on their input. She hired an attorney, but her case was dismissed because her attorney didn't file the necessary briefs to the people involved. An appeal was attempted, but due to not sending all the necessary papers, it was up for dismissal also. Dora died, succumbed to breast cancer; she didn't get to see justice. That is why it is important to fight until you can't fight. If you feel that a lawyer didn't do his or her job representing you, file a grievance against them. Go online. There are grievance forms and the address to whom you can address your complaint.

Well, we filed a grievance, sadly, the Grievance Committee ruled in favor of the attorney. All he did was reply to the grievance saying he made a mistake and the grievance department dismissed the grievance. I should've known but God has the final say. Well, I was inspired to write these two poems.

Here a poem I wrote after I went to a Council's meeting.

Majority Rules by JJB

Appeasing my contingents, I didn't return your calls
I'm a council member now
But what about my sister's plights
Sorry! My conscience states it's not my fight
I'm the one who spoke at the City Council Meeting
Yes!
You seemed angry!
A little ghetto, I'll say
Something in your face seemed so familiar
However, I dare not say
Wow! Did you just say, you're
"An Angry Black Woman"
My contingents face turned a shade red
I wanted to crawl under the table
Especially when you stated that, we need to get off our behinds
And look into this matter
Your philosophy was bold
Then after the meeting,
Hey girl,
Don't I know you?
I did not recognize you at first; we worked together
So, true, you stated,
It's me, the person that spoke on my sister's

behalf
Yes, I know you, call me, my phone no. It's in the book
Call…
Hey! I'm running behind
Will call you back
Waiting...
Called again, left messages
Nah, Nah, she didn't'
Now, it seems clear
When we voted you in
You had all good intentions
I'll be the "go to person," as you stated
Should've known
Emailed you, before the city council meeting
No response
Called twice after
In your speech when you're trying to get elected
You seemed so sincere
Was it just a ploy?
You said one thing
For the people
After getting elected,
Now, your voice danced to a different note,
Sitting among the elite
I'm with the majority now
Your action dictates
"Majority rule"
Even though my skin color is different from the majority,
I've switch sides; you smiled, a Kinta grin,
To appease my fellow council members

Majority rules, don't tell the nice people who voted me in
They thought they had a good nigger but I was a closet Kinta, with a grin

We are the people written by JJB

What does it mean?
To say, "We are the people," means:
There will be a fair and just representation, no remorse
Or puffed up pride.
To say, "We are the people" means:
I will not let my counterpart slay me or intimidate me.
To say, "We are the people" means:
I will stand tall as a man/woman amongst my peers and
Be judged fairly
And not dismissed because of my title.
To dismiss me means to dismiss you.
My soul cries out for justice when the scales that are depicted
Are blindfolded.
So what do I do? I look up and pray, God please tip the scales my way.
I ask you again, what is the meaning of we *are the people?*
Don't be intimidated my child.
Walk tall, whatever the title, whatever the means.

You are equal, my child, not by percentage or worth
That men/women hold so precious but lack the commodity of love.
"We are the people" represents all men/women:
Janitors, factory workers, machinists, lawyers, doctors, day care
Workers, teachers, athletes, social workers, nurses, office workers,
Judges, authors, writers, etc.
All people make up the world. To shun one, means to shun us all
"We are the people" means no matter how high you climb the corporate
Ladder or how humble the means, we should have the same fair
Representation and not be dismissed along the roadside as weeds.
"We are the people," means we all must be represented fairly and
Justly. This, my friend, is the hope that we all strive for; this
Delicacy is a fruit for us all to live and prosper in peace.

Now, my sister's story is out there and sadly her story isn't an isolated incident.

Thinking, I was zealous in my efforts, but when it doesn't concern whomever, then it's just an effort. Let us pray, Dear God please let this be the last time this happens, step in and quiet their thoughts of corruption, you have the power. Dear

God; don't let them destroy any more lives, that come their way. Let them know, that a higher power has intervened, and justice is in your hands, in Christ name I pray!

Justice for My Sister

There came a time to forgive after thinking about my sister's situation. If someone was cold hearted enough to do this to her, wouldn't you pity them? I pray to God to stop efforts on their part to convict people without a proper investigation. Why would anyone convict someone knowing that they didn't do the crime; it's a tragedy. Thank God, I have a conscience that dictates what's right and what's wrong. With pressures from each end of my life, there is hope. The spirit of love for my family motivates me to forgive. It is an act of evilness to cause a person to lose their job, especially when they are fighting for their life, but evilness does exist. Coming out of my naïve state, I questioned the justification to destroy others. Why do people destroy others just for the sake of corruption? What have I done to correct the injustice against my sister? Well, here are some things I have done. First, I went and spoke to the Chief of Police who was polite. While I was there, my niece called and we both discussed my sister's plight. He told me that he had just come from viewing the tape. When I left, I had a feeling that another thing had been swept under the rug. When my sister called the Chief, she stated he was rude to her, saying it seemed that she was talking in circles. After thinking about our strategy, my sister and I went and filed two complaints against the officers at the Police Dept. The officer she spoke to, Mr. K., stated that the complaints against the two officers were already on file. Then she asked to see the complaints. He stated that he couldn't let her <see the complaints, but Mr. K. told her to fill out another complaint. Odd, we thought. In the meantime, another one of our sisters came to the police department and spoke to the officer's supervisor. After speaking to the supervisor, she told Dana to speak to Ms. L. Dana called back and stated this to Mr. K that she wanted to speak to his supervisor., but he got annoyed. From the tone of his voice, he was upset., plus this dark-skinned man, probably, turned even darker. "Bring the paper back to me," I heard him yell on the phone because I was nearby to hear the whole conversation.

Going home, I thought about the way the people at the police department were treating my sister. That night I wrote a letter to Mr. K, telling him that he treated my sister badly. This letter informed him that he needed to respect my sister as a law-abiding citizen, because my sister had never been in any trouble with the law. I also told him, "Don't get it twisted, you are black all day long, Mr. K." It was unbelievable the way our so-called police officers and detectives treated D. They acted as if they were above the law and not officers for the people. Dana was a law-abiding citizen, not a thug off the street. Working all her life, Dana had never taken a year off since graduating from high school. If this could happen to her, it could happen to anyone, I thought. These were gloomy days; the thought of getting out of bed was a struggle for my sister. It was very hard for me to watch someone suffering, as I saw her spirit dismantle.

The sheriff fired my sister with no write-ups in her file and no stated reason. Why did anyone give one person this much authority? It was so weird. Finally, it was time for Dana and me to file a grievance letter to the sheriff's department. Oddly, the receptionist said that there weren't any grievance forms. Tired, my sister gathered her strength and wrote one out. Since D wasn't feeling well, she sent the complaint by me to give to the sheriff. I marched in like a soldier and gave it to the neat looking man with a kind looking face. Did this man just fire my sister? It was hard to believe but it happened. While working, my sister had lost 300 hours. That was time she had saved to deal with her illness, breast cancer. It was cold on their behalf to take away her livelihood, but people don't care these days; it seems that self-gratification is what counts. All the people involved with this firing should be ashamed. But why was she being treated so unfairly? Sadly, it could be you! If this was an isolated incident, it would be different, but searching the Internet, lets us know that this has become prevalent in our society—authority and law enforcers abusing their power.

Getting off the subject . . . there are other problems facing so many Americans. If you see someone in trouble what will you do! Will you help them? Let me tell you something--I was literally falsely lied on, due to helping someone that no one else wanted to help or get involved with. This is for real. Helping someone in trouble can sometimes be the worst mistake you could ever make in your life; that's why people don't get involved. So many people become detached from society, and it's because they have been burned.

In my sister's case, she refused to lie and was fired. She was fired for literally no reason because corrupt officers wanted her to lie. Sad! Corrupt officers planting and tampering with evidence is widespread. We don't need more people in jail for something they truly didn't do! False confessions are shameful. But do the corrupt care? They sit in the churches and other places of worship professing to be Christian, not caring about the innocence gone due to their hands. How can someone teach their children values when they themselves are guilty of crimes? Well, let me move on. Don't you feel sad for them! I couldn't sleep if I did something to hurt someone. Now, some people might ask if this is real. Sure! Most of us know someone who has gone through some of the things talked about in this book. They mourn in silence because it hurts. The abuse robs you of happiness. For me, it took years to simply let someone hug me, I didn't know if the hug was genuine or not. It's scary. Afraid that people would find me out was always a struggle. Affectionate gestures frightened me because my abusers used this to trap me. Were there strikes against me before I was born, sometimes I wonder! Lately in life, there has been one pet peeve in my family that irritates me--its religion. What I have to say is don't judge your family members because of religious preferences they might have chosen. In my family this has happened too many times. At the end of the day, your family members will be the one who swipe your butt, not the sisters in the church

or congregation. Sure! You might get some money here and there or friends might bring over some food. But if you isolate yourself from family because of their faith, you'll eventually wonder if your actions are just. There have been numerous occasions when my family had gatherings and I didn't know anything about them until they were over. Now, this is surely not the Christian way. My siblings were not concerned about the isolation or hurt feelings; at the end of the day, all they cared about was appeasing their friends of faith. Being a member of a particular religious group doesn't mean the person will practice the religion. If the truth were told, you probably would be shocked. There is a vital point I would like to make: Please don't judge your family member by their religious preferences because this will come back to haunt you later on in life. This has happened in my family. It hurt my feelings, but they thought they were justified in their actions. Your family is your lifeline; don't people have a clue? God didn't discriminate so why should you? If you are a Christian, people will respect you as such. Now, did my siblings act like they were Christian? No! What I really thought about my sisters were that they were missing all the things they had been taught. If a person has any understanding, shouldn't they know right from wrong! GG belongs to their faith, but have they taken the time to go and see her? No! I have a life, but I went! People don't think until they get into trouble. Oh well, that's life.

Mother regaining strength

My mother has done a 100 percent turn around. One time she wasn't eating or talking; now she is fussing if things don't go her way. It's a blessing to hear her talk. The brick walls I felt in my way have been lifted; only God knew the strength and weakness. He knew I was at the breaking point and he intervened. I know this personally because of the overwhelming feeling deep down in my heart that was tearing me apart.

Getting back to my mother . . . Later in life my mother seemed to be a functional person. In the past she had different bouts (short periods) with depression, but now, she maintains her sanity. Years have passed and there have been no breakdowns, thanks to God. Recovering from two knee surgeries, she is sane with demands: do this, do that. Finally, there is a sign of relief, because this woman has really been sick. We didn't know if she was going to make it or not. Mr. Ed's health, on the other hand, is in question. He grunts all day long. If a person has a breathing problem, as he has, why smoke? It's stupid. I would never smoke if I had trouble breathing. Poor Dad, he's been an alcoholic and smoker all his life. Even older, Daddy forgets Mother can't pick up after him anymore; he still throws paper, clothing and food everywhere. He isn't tidy the least bit. An old saying I heard goes, "You turn back into a child when you get older," so sure! When your parents get older, the roles are reversed; the children take on the parents' roles. But as I think back, my father never picked up after himself; it was my mother's job, he said. Daddy was from the old school: the man went to work and the woman stayed at home and cleaned the house.

As the aging process continues, it affects everyone. My parents are both disabled now, and the routine of daily care is a struggle. Looking after them has become a challenge. But you know, when things get out of hand, God always comes knocking. I remembered, 'my gas had ran out' (a slang expression meaning, I felt I couldn't take any more bad news). Then, my mother made a recovery--she started back eating and talking. Thank God, because I didn't know what to do. It was a miracle! Don't ever give up in time of trouble. God's word will stand! Being a trusting person, my husband, paid a man to cut down some trees; he signed a hand-written contract with the man and his wife. Take in mind, the man never listed contact information or his last name. Well, we had sixteen trees to be cut down; the stumps were included in the price the man quoted to my husband. When my husband told me about the deal with the tree contractor, I told him to get his license, his phone number and other information where the man could be reached. My husband fussed me out, saying the man will not do him wrong. I told him, "Well, if anything goes wrong, you better deal with it then." He didn't know the man from Adam. First, the man told my husband the work would be done in about a week, but the work dragged on for weeks and weeks. The yard was a mess; tree branches were everywhere. Our yard looked awful! People started stopping by and asking when the man was going to finish the job in our yard. My husband didn't have an answer. Then one day, my husband asked me did I get the man's telephone number and information on the man's whereabouts. "No!" I yelled. "Since you would not listen to me at first, it's your job to find out that information." Eventually, the man returned; he worked hurriedly trying to complete his tasks. There are too many "curve balls, in life. Looking out the window on a cold night, I asked myself what is more precious than money? Family!

Nothing but pennies in my pockets, I'm content. Having a place to live and people who love me, isn't that what counts?

Sometimes my thoughts drift back and forward. I frequently question myself and ask if anyone is sincere anymore. We live in a world filled with 'get or get got.' There is little loyalty. Why can't we just love each other? Isn't there enough love to go around? Just give love, but there are too many fools out there. People just don't care.

Freedom

Freedom, where is the voice?
Men have risked their life for this word
But what is freedom?
Freedom! Freedom!
What a powerful word?
On the backs of common slaves struggling to be free
So many tears, they fought hard to be heard
From the wise man raising his hand high in the sky
To the young baby thirsting for milk
To deny one is to employ another
That's what it's all about
Freedom is an indemnity (insurance) that can't be bought or trade
Freedom is an entity (article) that protects us from greed and

Deception. It is an entitlement (power) that can't
be bought
Or procured (obtain)
Freedom is the opportunity to say
I am what I will be
Untamed, Uncultivated, but I'm free

Epilogue

What happen to Josie? Well, she got married; had three children. Josie divorced her first husband and married for the second times. She later preceded to go back to school and get an Associate Degree in Medical Assisting. Josie also, is the author of four books.

Josie thinks titles are overrated because a person worth shouldn't be based on their titles, but for her audience, she felt the urge to let them know that even with the odds not in her family favor, they rose from darkness to pivot their way to change the world with their valuable contributions. Josie along with her siblings have went on and achieved their dreams despite their unstable history.

Occupation: RN, Captain in the US Army, Respiratory Therapy, MA, Apostle, NA, and PCA. It was hard, but they fought amidst a world that said they couldn't, to yes I can!

If you take anything from this book, remember this, words can be a building block or a stumbling block, so be careful what you say because "once said, words can't be taken back, they only travel one way. My nephew, Jamey Wilkins wrote a poem, *One Way* that elaborates on this. When you call other people names, reflect on the hurt and pain you are inflicting on someone. Is your family without flaws? I don't think so. With drugs, with abuse, mental issues and other factors in our lives, no family is immune. Try to treat people with respect. Because, the times we are living in, it's hard, but remember that your attitude could break someone's spirit, and I'm sure you don't want to do that.

My life has been an uphill battle, but with the help of a higher power, I'm a survivor. People will be rude and feel they are justified to act a certain way. Even if you do manual labor, try to respect others! One of the greatest men that ever walked this earth was called names, but he held the key to life for all -- Jesus Christ.

Did you learn anything from reading this book? It was my desire to help shed some light on Josie's struggle to rise above mental abuse, physical abuse and poverty, as she matured into a woman. Now for those out there who think this book is too personal, let me say this: there are so many people out there with similar stories. If this book can help one person, it would fulfill my aspirations. It would be a small price for someone's empowerment. Hopefully, someone will realize his or her own potential. Reading this book could be a therapeutic adventure for others. Remember that there are so many stories out there that need to be told. Also, for others it may serve as a remedy. If life "throws you a curve ball," don't let it dictate your fate. This was a ride and I hope you enjoyed it; now that you are educated, what are you planning on doing? If you are a bully, suffering from mental or physical abuse, get help! Choose a life that will only allow you the luxury of growing. If some of the things mentioned in this book have happened to you, don't be embarrassed! Take charge of your life! Run to a better space and just know sometimes when people do get involved with other people's problems, there are bad consequences. That's why few people intervene.

After reading this book, I hope you will be inspired to become a mentor to a child or adult who may have mental health issues. Now you know to change your behavior or become an advocate for people suffering with mental illness issues. Don't let these people become misplaced without your passionate input. All my life, I have made it my business to help people in some small way; one small act of kindness could change the concept of how someone perceives his or her life. Ah, is this fact or fiction? You decide. Someone you know, or someone you will see, knows this little girl (Josie), a little girl just like me -- afraid, searching, hollering for help please, please, someone, please help me! **Now, you might wonder which parts unreal and which parts are real. I will leave that alone any say whether it's the little girl, Josie, in this story or someone close to you, don't put shades on when the truth is right in your face; just believe. This story has happened and it's time for someone to tell. Is this your story as well? This book also represents all the positive people in my life. Without their encouragement, this book would not have been possible.**

So, before you point a finger, look within your circle of friends and family members and search your heart deep to find out what you can do. If you can help one child or person in need, you will get your rewards with smiles instead of tears. **So with every deaf ear closed, there will be many lives that will be lost.**

Another poem in memory of Little Butterbean, my grandson

Little Butterbean Resting

Beneath the stem of the rose, there was a tear,
I gazed and was startled. I'd seen this tear before
Could it be my little butterbean?
But once again my heart sank in my chest
I have been through this so many times
God is this a sign, certainly you know all my
needs
One day the plan will be in place
Little butterbean will rest gently in my arms
And the little droplet of tears amongst the stem
of a rose
Will be placed amongst my chest, to blossom
into a seed
Sprouting from the seeds of an angel. Smiling,
there stood
My little butterbean
Love you. Always remember, Mother, God loves
us more, not less than before
He understands your pain, in order for his plan
to be in place, there will be pain
There will be heartaches, but remember mother,
these hardships will not last
Don't cry! Mother dear
God heard your silent tears; he knew your love
meant a lifetime to me

Your heart will be filled one day, filled of love, because I believe
I believe my Heavenly Father, and his words are the light and the truth
Toward the end of my journey to complete this book, I found out firsthand how people are struggling to overcome mental illness and trying to live a productive life but they are still looked down on, even by their own family. Mental illness isn't a dirty little secret or anything to be embarrassed about; it's an epidemic that affects so many lives. Belittling or making fun of someone shows that you are just plain uninformed. Anyone can have a breakdown due to crises that are going on today: unemployment, food-shortage, a single-parent household, a family crisis, mental abuse, physical abuse, etc. This is a thought for you.

Empowerment Pages for Gifted Poets

Pain! The Manifestation Of Hurt by Jamey Wilkins

When the break starts
The ache starts
At the exact juncture where love ends
Hate starts
But first comes the hurt
Which eventually change
Into pain
That can't be felt on the physical plane
Just as some sights
Are beyond our visual range
Visible scars can't determine
The existence of pain
It's the manifestation of the hurt
That was birthed from a throb
That began with the ache
From the break of a heart
Which is different from the break of a bone
That'll hurt because of the pain
From the second is the injury
The first in the brain, the ache will only throb
Until that injury's sealed, but in the first place
You will have to be mentally healed
Which takes time
The impatient have to stubbornly wait
And walk the thin line
That divides the love and the hate
When dealing with the heart
Be smart think first with ya brain
Or you'll have to endure
The breaks, aches, hurts and the pain

The Potential for Greatness by J.Bridgers

When I was a child, I wondered
What was so deep in my soul that made me daydream?
As I reminisced, I think of the word my momma use to say
"Child never mind what people say
You have the potential for greatness
You are my child prodigy can't be written off
So many women have been beaten and cursed
Until their broken bodies surrendered to the callings of the wild
But endure, my child, the taunts, and the snares placed in your path
Raise your head!
Keep on spitting forward greatness with every
Prolific verse of speech written and spoken by men
You are the product of greatness,
Birthed from pain and received with opened hands
A beautiful child
You are that little girl that rose from the gates of hell to reclaim
What others mocked and tried to destroy
Keep your head high!
Sometimes greatness come with a price
Look my child
I hear the call from the wilderness
Claim your path now before the lions tear you apart

Who are you my child?"
My name is (your name) and I
Have the potential for Greatness!

Sometimes we got to struggle and go through things to understand the blessings we already have

Your breath is my breath by JJB

You're my breath of life,
Your intoxicating smile is the theme to all my rhythms and poems
You legitimized my love, allowing me to mirror positivity
Your awe-inspiring persona allows me to jump over any obstacles giving me super human strength to persevere and regain more strength to battle the climate of time.
Sightless, blinded by your intoxication, I jogged on an escapade trail to an unreal lane
This mysterious path to the valley of sweet tender notes of silhouette shadows, captivates my curiosity and allures me on
I see shadowy figures surrounded by waves and notes floating in the air while an enthusiastic soul played Summer Rain
Such poetic meaning of expression you have given me, intriguing me, you speak with such poetic lyrics. These moments are captured on the tip-topes of the moon's smile in the bliss of the night. Intensifying the scenery of bliss, squirrels assembled to steal pears form an overflowing tree.
While the dog slept unshaken, leaving the trees vulnerable for the squirrels to stack the deck. We laughed; as we stared into each other's eyes while taking in the scent of the moon's fragrance, this

delighted all our senses in the breeze of the midnight heat.
A night my breath regained its strength, while every minute I savored the smell of your minted breath, redeeming my yearning to be close in the presence
A time when only a second, time allured the chase of morning. Then night waited for dawn in ecstasy and delight
Surely, I thought, the ideology of living is invigorating
Then all thoughts ceased
As the Sun rose to a new day

This Black Roses
symbolizes
My Love for you
If you've ever experienced
any type of pain

"Or walked a mile in my
shoes"

"When you give up, you give your power to someone else"

What is it if Not...written by Shaklera Middleton

Life
What is it not a meaningless game?
Love
What is it if not a torturous flame?
Lust
What is if not a painful addiction?
Birth
What is it if not a repeated tradition?
Fate
What is it if not a predetermined will?
Death
What is it if not a sardonic buzz-kill?

Infinity written by Shakiera Middleton

Infinity too long to go on
Sleep nowhere to be found
Through the looking glass
Soon an ugly mass
One token for gratitude
Two falls from grace
Night incenses your attitude
Red seeps down your face
Under the dirt and grime
The sound of truth lies in the mind

MOMMY written by Shakiera Middleton

My Mother was a Guardian Angel
She protected us no matter what
My Mother was a Saint
She loved us and cared for us when we couldn't do it ourselves
My Mother was a savior
She saved me more than once in many ways
My Mother couldn't help but love everybody
And we couldn't help but love her back
My Mother forgave no matter how bad the circumstances
She still loved you
My Mother will always be in my heart
I love you MOMMY

Random by Shakiera Middleton

Daydream of a Thousand Suns
Grass so thick like Green beans
Flighty little Gnome stalks your every move
Age-old traditions
Cage cold conditions
Daydream of Thousand Suns
Thrifty fingers
Fire lingers
Unsightly Chiappet
How much do you bet?
Daydream of Thousand Suns
Eye catching flower
Big Black Man insane with desire
Colorful heartbeat
Work, Work, Work consumed by the heat
Daydream of a Thousand Suns
Yellow light shifting from the flames
Poor Carpenter burns no remains
Parakeet obsolete
Cabbage it just won't eat
Brown Blob endearing as it may be
Protruding forms where will they be
Coffee beans are smoking. Ribbons for choking.
Rain Pollutes deep Daydream of a Thousand
suns

"Hate has no place to receive goods"

I want to Live by JJB

I want to take in the majestic glory of his words
Swallow up the scent of his mercy
See the Love embedded on his forehead
To believe glory is the majestic works of the All Mighty
Where he places the delicacy of his fruits of eminent wisdom on
Clouds filled with intrinsic love that breathes hope
Just to know God
Has destroy pain
through his giving mercy from his heart
He planted the seeds of our redemption and the ***Bible*** gives accounts of his loving kindness
Through Jesus Christ name
Everlasting is not far away

Heartfelt Memories JJB

Into our hearts an angel was born, she sprouted from
A rose to wrestle the waters to guide us
From a world filled of thorns
Heartfelt love she poured out to all she knew
Guarded by faith
Guarded by moments of memorable times
Of a life of laughter that resonated when she smiled
Just a phone calls away, no matter what time of the day
To let us know how much she cared,
As time grows near, we salute her life
For the times she was sad for less than a minute
A rapture of laughter embodied her face
Mother, your love was authentic, but what was so special about you mother dear you gave what you could to the people you knew. I know your burdens were heavy much more than we could imagine
But with a gesture of hope, we gave you our love
Thank you mother for your undying love
We recognized you as the positive rock in our lives
Although we are saddened for such a great lost
Your Love for us will remain unwavering in our minds and hearts

Life is hard but living and loving are extremely harder.

***

Why do I cry written by Josephine J. Bridgers

Lady: Come here little boy
Why are you crying?
Boy: Maam I'm crying because I'm hungry
Over yonder, I've lived the pities of poverty
Look at my fingers! They're bruised from digging
The filth of the earth for food
Naw my child, no
Boy: why have ya'll cast me aside
Lady: reaching out to comfort child
Lady Speaking: Children yall don't know the
poison of poverty.
The hurt that has cursed this child's lips from
HUNGER
In a society that has reversed the rule of Law
To Love each other with passion and honor
Are we in competition with our enemies to starve
our children?
Boy: Mama my burdens are heavy but there are
others with "a pill to swallow" bigger than mines
that's why I cry
I cry because the fruits they have been given are
filled with venom.
Lady: Come here child we will cry together, there
will be no careless expression of emotion
because I feel your Pain
Child: But mama, I'm afraid to let my shame be
exposed
(Someone in the audience calls the boy a coward)
Oh yes, to be called a coward
Yes, I face that fear every day

won't let fear bruise my ego or tarnish my conception of life
So I cry
Lady: I cry too my child because I'm tired, tired of all the opposition
Why is no one alert to see this child is hurting?
Please someone reach out and touch his pain. My pleas go out for this little boy. Tomorrow it might be your child
Will the anticipation of tomorrow be better?
Oh yes, because tomorrow I will stand in the midst of the poverty
And wrestle my way to freedom to save this child.

I Am a Man by Josephine Jenkins Bridgers

Blood bathed in tears, it seems like decades ago. They have walked in the shadows of the ones that had become before me, screaming for fairness, as they roamed the streets, covered in sheets.
They are cowards because they put on a disguise; let them stand as a man for their beliefs, without coverings up their hate with white sheets. I walk steady and firm because I am who I say I am, a **Man**.
What constitutes a Man, why am I still considered a boy? If I walk like a man, let me be what I am, a **Man**.
Why do you call me out of my name, if I don't have the strength to work longer hours, when I am aching, and my body is sore?
Why can't I ride my Mercedes along the road, without being stopped and interrogated for hours or so?
Why am I considered less of a man because I dare to challenge the ill fate of my brothers, who were falsely accused and now live a life behind bars, for what they truly don't know? Can't I rest for a while, without people staring, accompanied with the sound of a sirens, when I walk out my door. Why can't I move into your neighborhood without pressure from my friends fearing I am not who I am
All I ask, all I want, is to be a Man

They tried to break me written by JJB

Stamped on. Tramped on.
They tried to break me
But I have something
Something they can't take
I have the power of thoughts
This indefinable present
God has endowed in my spirit
One man
No power
A Supreme Court Ruling
Please
Now, my friend who is the fool?

There're sending me to Super-max by JJB

They are sending me to Super-max
Robbers, Murders, they didn't send
But me, they want to silence my voice
Why, the power of the spoken word
Has cause them to retaliate
But I'm not going to blame them
Because there will be others just like me
Not broken
Smiling
Saying; 'Jamey paved the way for our voices
And to that my friend, we are extremely proud.

Death alludes me JJB

The Salty taste of death
Delights my tongue
It seduces me
Taunting me
Like weeds consuming
Rose seeds
Ah
The earthy rhythm
Dancing around and around
Calling me, come
Alas it is morning
While the morning is overshadowed by night
Tasting the salty taste of death on my palate
numbs
My tongue
Suddenly light embodies my presence
Every time I have embraced the icy stings
Of death
My weaknesses
sends it away
Come I will go without a fight
Then the light overpowered the darkness
Crushing the sting of death as I awaken from my
sleep to a new day

The Man is holding me Down
by Stanley Griffin

My brothers are locked up
And they want let them out
It was bondage back in the day
But the man has slowly removed bondage
And replaced it with ignorance
Who is the man?
Is he white?
Only the person being held down knows that.
Whose got their hands on your back, my brother?
Oh that's right you said it was the man.
Who knows who the man is?
Can somebody tell me so that I can help my brother get up?
I'm coming to help you my brother.
But what can you do for yourself until I get there?
Can you hold the man off?
Is the man so strong that you can't think?
Is the man so strong that you won't try?
Holding the man off determines whether you live or die!
So tell me my brother can you do that for yourself?
What? Yeah can you hold the man off?
Who is the man I say?
Can anyone tell me who the man is?
Is he white?
I need to know who that damn man is.
I can't help my brother unless I know who he is

I'm talking about the man who has my brother down.
Who saw him what does he look like?
Is the man educated?
Nah! He can't be educated because he has my brother down.
And educated man can't be held down.
So now I know.
He is not an educated brother who has my brother down!
Educated brothers help themselves and their brothers.
So I ask this question again. Is he white?
No! Who said that?
It is I. Who?
Myself.
What
Yes, it is I who holds my brother down.
Who is I?
Me
Hey man you confusing me,
Me not confused it is me who is holding me down
You telling me that I am holding myself down,
I thought that you'd get it.
Get what?
Get the answer to who the man is.
Who is the man?
Ok you said that the man is holding you down right?
Right!
Alright look there.

Look where?
There in that mirror.
Who do you see?
Me. Whose hand is that
Mine.
My brother please takes your hand off of your
back and get the hell up!

Sometimes the façade is more than what you see

Let's Get Acquainted written by Jamey L. Wilkins

Cool people embrace me but schooled people hate me. I use people, so only a few people can escape me. You can't shape me, can't mold me, or control me. I have one mission and that is solely to destroy all that is holy. I've been applied to many guys. I am genocide in disguise. Men/Women devised a scheme now their dreams are being materialized.

Who am I? Ha! Ha! Ha! I am the one you least expected. The one you yearn to have sex with, with whom you'd never use protection. Hold up.... I have a confession.... I just lied! It is not who or where I am for I cannot be characterized.

I am brawny, I am scrawny, I am white, I am black. I am comely, I am homely, I am this, I am that. I am here, I am there, I am lovable, and hatable. I'm in a polygamous relationship so I am always available, from homosexuals to bisexuals to heterosexuals. The only ones who are questionable are the "I don't have sexual."

Pardon the intrusion, sorry if I've caused confusion, but let me start with the problem and conclude with the solution. It is hard to avoid me seeing that the media is collusion. Unbeknownst to them, of course, are the strategic methods that I'm using. I mingle amongst the "in crowd". I blend in with the stars. The people kids idolize transport me like cars. They take me to your T.V. screens and magazines, cause "sex sells." As evidenced in commercials and the classified section of your XXL"s. They promote me, if you ain't having sex, you aint cool. So once virginity is lost, kids brag about it in school. A bunch of fools, I lure them and majority bites the bait, which exponentially increases the chance of putting their life at stake. My goal is to conquer the globe, but I have to move fast to accomplish it. Condoms slow me down but abstinence is more abstinent. I'm so intelligent I use a different tactic for the celibate. I run rampant in poverty-striven environments where crime and drugs are prevalent. Family problems leave them depressed, it gets stressful through the years. While they are some sort of solace I offer pressure from their peers. It seems the only way to escape the madness is through liquor and wee. That's just the beginning so it really doesn't make a difference to me. Eventually they'll drop their drawers... with luck they'll drop their drawers, if not, that's okay I'll let fate take its proper course.

Addiction. The same dosage no longer gives them a buzz. So to achieve their high they change the way that they administer drugs. First they smoked it, then they sniffed it, anything to get lifted. Now I recruit their friends to introduce them to something different. It's just a needle prick, it won't hurt, it may bleed a bit. But it's the quickest way to get high, when you need a fix." And to fit in they just allowed me to enter them, gave me permission to use their body as my instrument.

Simpletons.... after I am injected, I remain undetected. By the time I show my face they won't know when or where they were infected. I possess them. Rejection...feelings of depression inspires some to intentionally transmit me to the next man/woman.

Beautifully we enter the club with a fake I.D. Now that we're partners, let's get acquainted, "Hi I'm H.IV."

How to protect yourself? That's a secret I wouldn't normally give away. But I learned that the majority is ignoring me anyway. Some feel that I exist but won't happen to them. They are so naive and that's why I'm attracted to them.

If you have to have sex I'd suggest you use a condom. I rarely breach the barrier, latex always give me a problem. To be 100% sure obtain from intercourse totally. Then it's virtually impossible for you to be sexually exposed to me. Or you could find a partner, take the test, and practice monogamy. If your partner decides to cheat... well I offer you my apology.

The abuse of drugs will alter your mind state. Often it puts you in a coffin or increases the crime rate. No drugs, no blood, no me. We would never get acquainted and you would never get to know me.

But you will see me because I am a slow death imperialized. Without you, though, some men/women dream cannot be materialized. You are schooled so now you hate me, while cool people still embrace me. I've used people but you are one of the few people who escaped me… for now

*"People sometimes come as a friend
Beware, be mindful because trust
belongs to the ones earning it!"*

"Swallow up your pride
Just apologize"

A Dream sometimes starts with an inch

What makes it bigger is the power of hope

Bully-Proof written by Jamey L. Wilkins

I have a vest on one that the good Lord has given me
It is not made of Teflon
But honor, respect, and dignity
It protects me from the taunts
The stares, calling me a 'freak' ("creep")
So you can pick all you want
It doesn't affect me in the least
Physically you may bruise me
But mentally I am blessed
Verbally you abuse me
Which proves you don't have a vest
So I am not mad at you
For looking for a fight
Actually I feel sad for you
And hope you get a life
You appear to be stronger, richer, taller
In much better health
But to me you are weaker, poorer, smaller
Not content with yourself
That's why you're a Bully

Why Should I Care written by Jamey L. Wilkins

If for me there is no profit
Or nothing I could lose
Why should I care?
When someone else is abused
I eat well; sate my thirst
My pockets are filled with money
So why should I care
If a child is going hungry
I am physically fit
I have no allergies or bad habits
Why should I care?
That so and so is a crack addict
I'm smart, well employed
Life to me has been sweet
Why should I care?
If that old lady can't cross the street
No worries for me or mine
No reason to go out on a limb
So why do I care?
Because I could've been one of them

The Song, Grown Folk Love by Jamey L. Wilkins

Chorus: I want that Odell, Eddie, Josephine, Calvin, Dianne, Lonnie, only one out of a thousand unconditional love is what they known for' Let's bring that ♩ old thing back ♩ and love like them Grown Folk x 2

Verse 1: I wish I had the love of a woman like my grandmamma to my grandfather
Stuck together, never left him even though he had problems
Wit' that bottle, see a lot of women make a quick decision
Say they love you but the only thing they loving is the feeling
That you give'em but that feeling only caught'em for a minute
When you finish, they notice all ya flaws and see ya blemish
That's the difference, in these caliber women
They don't limit ya challenges they challenge ya limits
And I know my shortcomings' a tall order
So if I find a lady that embraces me I would give my all for her
But nowadays we got coward ways, and hate our spouse
Where did the love go? Why did we forsake (break) our vows?
Cause we never mean'em, we were caught up in the moment

Now we talk with venom, cause this aint really what we wanted
And all I want, is my own woman
Someone that is a friend through thick and thin I need a Grown Woman
♪ Chorus x 2 ♪
Verse 2
  I need a woman I don't want a girl
Cause they know back in the old school "irreconcilable' won't a word
If it's worth having you should work for it, and when you finally get it
You should be willing to work wit it
I committed half of my life searching
…hurting...healing…hurting
Trying to find that person
Perfect, sun kissed, red brown, light dark
Type smart with the right heart, got all of the right parts
A nice thought, or, is she only a dream
A vision, from the past, something I've never seen
Or am I trippin', maybe I met ya, if that's the case
Forgive me, I didn't see ya, you were right in my face
There's something in me that craves the feeling of love
A relationship, more than a kiss or a hug, A commitment so my own woman, not a girl not a cougar or seducer naw I need a grown Woman!
Chorus x 4

I Walk Alone written by Jamey L. Wilkins

No one sees when the tears fill to the brim
And leak from the corner of my eye
No one stares, is it because no one cares?
Or is this weakness normal for a guy?
With my head held low, I have nowhere to go
I watch my feet pummel the ground
I glance in no direction; I look for no affection
As my tears start tumbling down
Only I can taste the salty embrace
Of my liquid sorrow
My tongue goes numb as if it were stung
I don't savor the flavor; I swallow
My stomach fills with emptiness
Memories range from bitter to sweet
The thirst of my soul remains unquenched
So my spirit continues to weep
Who can smell the scent of despair?
Intermingled with the aroma of guilt
I noticed a mare that's nostrils did flare
And in his eyes I saw only contempt
The stench of failure pollutes me, engulfs me
I am alone, trouble seems to follow me
As if attracted by my cologne
If anyone says they feel my pain
Then I would tell you, at once, they lied.
For if it were true when I'm hurt and I'm bruised
Tell me, why don't they cry?
Loneliness touches me, caresses me
In the wee hours of the night
I feel remorse for choosing this course

But I can't change the past try as I might
Nobody hears the plip-plop of my tears
Though my ears detect every drop
The bass drum of my heart is missing its spark
And sounds like it's ready to stop
I scream out in frustration, I sob; I sniffle
I whimper; my whole body stiffens
Ashamed at my lack of control, I face the globe
But it seems as if nobody listened
They pay no attention to my condition
And I feel that this needs some explaining
I look to the sky to ask the Lord why, And that's when I realize it's raining

Friend "written by Clarence Smith (CJ)

I never look back…
Cause my friend is there
When I got stabbed in the back…
I didn't look back
When I got pushed from the back…
I didn't look back
When the police said freeze…
I looked back
Cause my friend was s'pose to be behind me
Come to find out he called the police on me
Come to find out he was the one who stabbed me
Come to find out he was the one who pushed me
I never looked back because my friend was there
Now I look over and across the courtroom
And he mouthed the words "what are friends for

Blessing or Curse written by CJ

26…26… A place I will only be once
For 365 days
Then I'll move on to 27…. I'm sad and happy
Happy because I made it past
The statistics mark… on my life
They said it was a fact
But I prove them wrong
I'm sad because I'm a year older
I'm really afraid of the future
So I daydream about the past a lot
When my sisters and me use to live together
Those was the good ol'days
We was deep in the struggle…damn
I'm sad because I'm there more of these days
Away from my family
Blessing or curse
Me makin' it through '06 and 07' when those
bullets missed
Was that a blessing and me being in
Prison the curse… my life is crazy
This world is crazy
So you tell me, Blessing or Curse

Detour written by CJ

Stay focus
Look ahead
Don't turn
Back hurt
Neck cramps

Knees ache
Fingers sore
Feet blistered
Stand firm
Hold ya head up
Come to find out
It was only a test
Just to see
If you would detour
The real can take anything

Real Love" written by Khamad (Alvin Douglas)

To find myself wanting to love
Desperately.
Waiting for the next
Emotional Ride
I search for love endlessly
Because of my addition to the
Emotional High
To know Love Intimately
As To know Love As
A Lie
But Need Love Honestly
Cause with Every Touch of Pain
I'm reminded that I'm
Alive...

"Empathy" written by Khamad (Alvin Douglas)

To say you love me,
Is to say Yu know me
In order for you to know me
You must first understand me
You must first understand yourself!
If you don't know yourself
Then how can you really love yourself
How can you say you feel my pain?
When I'm the only one left broken hearted out in the rain?
How can you say I'm weak for not standing tall?
When you haven't felt the blows that made me fall
So don't sneer at me cause I'm down today, unless you have felt the blow
Or understand the pain that only I know!
To know me and my Pain
You must first know the meaning of empathy!!
Empathy "is the ability to feel as another person feels,
To emotionally be where I am, even if you haven't had exactly
The same experience that triggered the emotion...
Without empathy, you should never say you feel my pain,
Because empathy is hard to fake...!

I hate hope by Jamey L. Wilkins

I hate hope
Hope is like a…
Sorta like an um….
See, that's another reason I hate hope right there
Because it won't let you tell anybody what it's like
Let me tell you why I hate it though
It's cause for some reason it never turns out how you expected
Majority of the time it'll let you down
But it's those few times
Those never happen again in a million years times
That revitalizes you
And stokes the dying embers
Until once again the fire of hope consumes you
Yeah, I hate that shit

Nose open by J L. Wilkins

Magnetically attracted
Unable to resist
The hypnotic suggestions
On the lips
Diversions are diverted
Distractions non-existent
Eyes give attention captured
An oasis in the distance
Pavlovian reactions
To the pitch of her voice
Decisions are made without the glimpse of choice

**Proof that there's no such thing
As a foolproof plan by JL Wilkins**

I tiptoe barefoot
Down the corridor of iniquity
Hoping God
Doesn't hear me sneak
For carnal pleasures
There is no measure
I wouldn't span
To reach it's peak
I've planned; I've plotted
I've schemed and strategized
Every single move I'd make
For at least a week
Then as soon as I
Get close to my prize
Out of the blue
The floorboard squeaks

The beat of a broken Drum by Romeo (Telemanchus Bess)

Love is an orchestra of emotions
A symphony of sincere feelings
And the repercussion of its percussion
Reveal the vibrant vibrations of living
So I strive to play its song
Or simply impersonate its melody
But the sound is just all wrong
From what love's rhythm is telling me
Therefore the instrumental of joy is doomed
Causing the completion of love's song to be jinxed
Because there's an instrument not fully in tune
Which is why the melody is not in sync
So now the conductor looking around I guess
To figure out where the flow is coming from
And if only she could listen within my chest
where she'd find the beat of a broken drum

The Meaning of Melody by Jamey L. Wilkins

Bombarded by a cacophony of shots
Police sirens, tires squealing
Flow together like a synchronized plot
As if they were part of a violent rhythm
I bop my head to the beat
Of the producer's production
Knuckleheads in the street
Think when they or shooting I'm ducking
Many curse words and threats are found
Interspersed in the lyrics of the song
Even silencers have a sound
But once you hear it you're gone
The listener must be objective
The message in the music is telling me
For each individual's perspective
Is what determines the meaning of melody

The Truth written by Jamey L. Wilkins

Something you may not want to hear
It may hurt
But being who I be
And knowing what I know
I have to tell you
Because the omission would be worse
I…Don't…Know… How…To…Love!
There, I said it
Hopefully
I won't regret it
You see I've been
Living a lie
Now that I've finally found
Someone that I could love
Someone that I want to love
And realize I can't love
My shortcomings have been revealed
So I want to wipe the slate clean
And start anew
Remember all the times
I told you
"I love you"
think about it
I never actually showed you
I love you
Because
I was faking
Seeking instant gratification
Now I've grown up
It's time for me
To own up

To my actions
Or lack there of
I don't want to disappoint you
With clumsy attempts
I want it to be real
I want it to be true
I want to be able to satisfy you if you need it
I want to say it and really mean it but the truth
is…I can't

Deserted Island written by Jamey L. Wilkins

Cast away
Stranded
Last man standing
So who am I to look to?
For understanding
I send out flares
But no one cares
My pleas are confined
To the island of my mind
No shoulder to lean on
No one to lift me up
So if I slip, I fall
And no one will pick me up
Forced to endure
The torrential rains of pain
Alone
Without shelter
This house is not my home
Bottled messages thrown
None return
I'd love company
Someone to comfort me
But no one has come for me
So I sit
I wait…
And silently ache

Five months and counting

Is there a such thing as unfelt pain
Or did I just coin a phrase
That really describes something already in existence
I just don't know the name of
This is the reluctant
Acceptance of death
Not my death, but the death of my mother (or maybe that was my death)
It's been exactly five months and this unfelt pain still persists
I mean it hurts, but how?
I cannot pinpoint where the pain begins
I can't tell the doctor enough about it
For him to prescribe a potion that cures it
All I know is it exists
And sometimes when I least expect it
It strikes
With the accuracy of an expert dart thrower
Just to remind me it is still there
Sharp
Fast
And above all very, very…painful

The Beholder by Jamey L. Wilkins

In you I see magnificence
A beauty unrestrained
So I'd rather watch
Than have you
Because then you might become ugly

Padded Cell by Jamey L. Wilkins

Voices without faces
Indistinguishable from imagination
Fantasy and reality are red and blue
Lenses I look thru to form the 3 dimensions
Of my solitary detention

Dead Batteries by Jamey L. Wilkins

All I hear is static
A repetitive buzz
No recollection
Of whatever it was
Forced to listen to
This monotonous drone
All alone
Now that my music (momma) is gone

Halitosis by Jamey L. Wilkins

The husk of my trust
Winnows away
In the breeze of the liar's breath

2morrow will never come by Jamey L. Wilkins

It's like God licked his fingers
And put out my match
The match that lit my candle
The candle that sparked the lantern
The lantern that illuminated my room
Now I'm forever cloaked in darkness
Pitch black filled with gloom
Unless the sun decides to rise

April shower by Jamey L. Wilkins

Sometimes I feel insignificant, like my existence has absolutely
No effect on the world. I am just a raindrop in on April
Shower rising, falling, spinning to each whim of the wind
Until finally I splash and cease to be I.

Why (Y) Wouldn't I (Part One) written by Romeo (Telemanchus Bess)

Y Wouldn't I, maybe solely because they are so different
You see why just wants to know while I will actually listen
Y wouldn't I, maybe simply because it is a vowel
And why could be the reason I plurally am in denial
Y wouldn't I, maybe because y begins you
While I is singular for we as my one word truth
So y wouldn't I maybe because y is so close to the end
While I depending on how it's used could be how a sentence begins Really y wouldn't I because why manifest a questions presence, while I usually participates in revealing a statement's essence Y wouldn't I, maybe because of Y's crocked ways
While I seem to consist of paths that all run straight
Y wouldn't I because why is for what reason or purpose for which objection

It's expressing a surprised discovery or recognition impatience's reflection
Y wouldn't I because I is me, my, mines and we united as one
It's an intransitive independent interest also known as one
Y wouldn't I? To tell the truth I honestly don't know
But if I did I'd tell you wouldn't I? But why I really don't know would I ask y they ask and to tell the truth no, I wouldn't, y? I mean I only ask to receive a better understanding of Y wouldn't I

Why (Y) Would I (Part two) written by Jamey L. Wilkins

Au contraire, mon fre're, we don't see I to I
For there are some instances where Y would I
Though I is a vowel along with A, E, O, and U
Sometimes y is too depending on the word you use
In the future Y wouldn't I but the present they can be
In the participle Y would I if you add an N G

Also in the past Y would Z indeed
Because all you would have to do is add an E D
Y has crooked ways; true, you did not lie
For Y is so crooked he sometimes impersonates I
But Y doesn't know that I stays in violence
Or he wouldn't steal his voice in hYena and hydrant
So Y would I, think about it, even in math we learned
That if Y is in my and my is I then y would I in algebraic terms
Y is a question but I is in question
So Y would I not acknowledge their connection

Would I Y as Y would I though I is always straight?
Yes because I is in Y deceiving the eye as a sideways H
Now Y is in you, which is vastly different from I
But that doesn't mean Y wouldn't I cause Y would I if you give it a try

Let's live our lives with the high regard for love and peace

Aint No Love Here written by Jamey L. Wilkins

Vacant
Sorry, we're closed
Out to lunch
Aint no love here
Got me twisted
Mistaken identity
Cause aint no love here
I don't care
How you feel
I'm care-less
No fear
Bare chest
So don't even stop
And window shop
Cause aint no love here
Sold out
If you looking for it
This the wrong place
Come with high hopes
Leave with a long face
It's some dreams here
It's some pride here
It's some pain here
I'm not sure what is here
But I know what aint here…

Whenever I think of your Face by JL Wilkins

Whenever I think of your face
I can't help but smile
All the love you gave me
When I was a child
Whenever I think of your face
I can't help but grin
Cause all the joy you make me feel
Just can't be held within
Whenever I think of your face
I can't help but laugh
At how you use to look at me
When I made you mad
Whenever I think of your face
I can't help but praise the Lord
Cause out of all the women on this earth
He blessed me to be yours
Whenever I think of your face
I just shake my head
Cause I can clearly hear your voice
"Clean your room, Make your bed!"
Whenever I think of your face
I see perfection; it's true
That we are one and the same
I am a reflection of you
Whenever I think of your face
I feel warmth inside
I feel your love envelop me
I feel a bunch of pride, whenever I think of your face
I can't help but cheer

Because as long as you stay in my heart or thought
I'll always have you near

All I can Say written by Jamey L. Wilkins

I don't want to just say, "I love you"
For some reason those three little words
Don't seem to be able to encompass the depth
The width, the height of my true feelings
They seem too shallow, too thin, to short
I'd rather show you I love you
I'd rather give you everything you ever wanted
I'd rather take you everywhere you've never been
To show you how proud and thankful I am for
you
But I can't
So I have to do the best I can
The only way I know how
And that's by saying
I love you

Sometimes we love hard, over-looking the tell, tell signs of our conscience

My World written by Jamey L. Wilkins

Far, far away in a galaxy
Where nothing is as it seems
The oceans are pink
And the moon is green
There is no such thing
As money or cars
Where planets have dreams
Of becoming a star
People can fly
Without capes or wings
Animal can talk
And plants can sing
Women run naked
Wild and free
Anyone can be
What they aspire to be
All is well
Nothing is bad
Everyone smiles
No one is sad, in my mind I'll find a way
To go before I lose it when others tell me it
doesn't exist, I tell them to prove it
When others tell me it doesn't exist

Sleepless Dream written by Alvin M. Douglas (Khamad)

What is it that has me thinking of you in this way?
Is it really night or is it still day?
Damn
I pray I'm not having them sleepless dreams again
Cause when I do, I always find myself think of you standing in the rain.
You, it was you I asked to be my wife, so we could be combines
But you being you, I should have known that you" decline
But why
Is it because you don't want to be confined?
If that's the case, then why did you say you'll always be mine?
I thought it was our future we were trying to design
So why do I feel the feeling you're ready to resign?
You were the only girl I ever loved so passionate
But you left my heart asunder…
Like some food you just ate
When it use to beat for you, until the point it sounded like thunder...
I only wanted to bring you wonders
Not be like the last nigga who tried to take you under

I know your loving the fact that you have me moaning over you
But its all good, you better enjoy seeing me down.
Cause you'll never hear my love scream
Unless I'm having another one of my sleepless dreams…

Resistance by Jamey L. Wilkins written by

Pressure is nothing
Pain is noting
Fear is nothing
Force is nothing
Hate is nothing
Struggling is nothing
Because, freedom is everything

Job's Decision written by Jamey Wilkins

Alas, Satan wherefore thou hast followed me?
Thy sickle hast cut off, driven away broken and scattered
My children
Even my day of distress has yet to end
Sayeth thou onto me
Giveth thyself to me
Curse and forsake thy Lord
For he has forgotten thee
Giveth thyself to me
Mine eyes harden as of stone'
Laughter drowneth the cry of pain
Surely, I sayeth, thou hast never met my Lord
The memory of he that formed me
Is everlasting
Pain and death shall cease one day
Though I pray for that day
I will not hasten it
Neither will I allow thee
To consume me without a fight!

It was you and it was me written by Khamad (Alvin Douglas)

It was you who I made cry
When you wanted things to work, but I fail to try
It was me who heart you tried to fry,
When you left me "high and dry"
It was you who I made feel pang
When I close the streets over you and started to bang
It was me who you made depress
When I found out you wasn't shit, but a devil in a Black dress!
It was you I had thinking we was together for a reason
Until you saw our love fading away like the end of a season
It was me who you made feel so up tight
While at the same time making me see the light
And through all this…
It was you who stayed blessed
Even though I always left you stressed!
It was you who stayed strong
Although I done you so wrong! It was you who told me to believe, even though you knew I wanted to leave. But in the end…was me who asked you to be my wife cause I now see how much meaning you bring into my life

On my Own by Khamad (Alvin Douglas)

My pride is smeared with dirt
Having love for a nigga sometimes hurt
On my own two feet I stand
You can always tell the difference
Between a coward and a man
Some nigga garbage
Why others are made of gold
Nigga! Still don't have their priorities straight
Even though they damn near forty years old!
Heart of a lion
And soul of a king
I'm all by myself I don't need no team!
Hopes and dreams I keep on pushing
Keep your eyes open because nigga! Keep something cooking
Ain't never scared, but I keep it humble
That's why I always stay on my feet whenever I stumble...!

Rehabilitation written by Jamey L. Wilkins

Yesterday
I saw a thug
Come to prison
Today I saw him get raped
Tomorrow, he'll leave a changed man

Buck written by Jamey l. Wilkins

Sorry but it's embedded in me
Too deep to be brought up
Buck!
Yeah, you know what I'm talking 'bout
That acid that traverses through the veins
And won't let you submit to chains
The will that adamantly refuses to budge
That numbs you in the midst of pain
Buck!
I got plenty of it
So when you say sit and I stand up instead
Know the only way I'll stop standing
Is if you break both my legs
Hard headed, Buck is the antithesis of intelligence
But even an idiot is better than a spineless jellyfish
Man up for your ideals! Fight! Even if you lose
A moral victory last longer than any man-made bruise
Buck fuels my inner inferno
Warms my tortured soul
Allows me to look in the mirror and makes my countenance glow
Buck!
Just a drop of it gives me power
To gladly accept death as a consequence
Of refusing to be a coward!

Bannana Puddin written by JL Wilkins

It never looked as fancy as those fancy as those magazine pictures, but I doubt those pictures could taste as good, just the right amount of vanilla wafers, not too many bananas, every time. I put a spoonful in my mouth, my tongue just went bananas. From a beat-up, dented, half rusted pan and a second away from expiring ingredients she could work wonders. It was like magic. That's the only logical explanation because other meal she cooked could remotely compare to her banana pudding. The memory makes my mouth water. Sometimes it seemed sloppy, sometimes it looked burnt, but every single time it was delicious. I sure to eat as much as I could as fast as I could just, so I could get more before it ran out. The crazy part was it only happened on rare occasions. She only made it when she felt like it and I never understood that. If it was for us, then why want she make it when we felt like it? I guess Aunt Josephine had to wait for more magic

Searching written by Ghaalib and Wazo (Jamey L. Wilkins)

I'm searching left
For what
My self
I'm searching right
For what
The so-called light
I'm in a losing battle
So I guess
I'll just follow the cattle
Like the sheep to a shepherd
Or the feet
'Of a leopard
So I guess
It's easy to spot me
Yet hard to stop me
From going where
I wanna go
From knowing what
I wanna know
The truth

How Can I say I'm your Brother written by Jamey L. Wilkins

How can I say I'm brother?
For you to even ask that question
Tells me that you've allowed another
To break our past connection
How can I say I'm your brother?
When at times I don't act brotherly
Maybe it's because
You have been acting stubbornly
How can I say I'm your brother?
Have you taken into consideration?
That I may have been blinded
Or even miseducated
Does that make me not your brother?
Brother I ask you why
Do you disown me?
Because we don't see eye to eye
How can I say I'm your brother?
It disappoints me and I hate it
But that does not change the fact
That we are related
How can I say I'm your brother?
You must not understand the word
Because for some reason
You believe "brother" is a verb
My actions do bit determine
If you are my brother
Blood is blood
Irregardless if I love ya
I can open your eyes

But I cannot make you see
Now let me ask you
Who are your brother if not me?
The one who shares your burdens?
The one who shares your color?
The one who shares your pain? That is me…my brother

Silencer by C. J (Clarence Smith)

Listen...noting
That's my point
The worst
You
Can
Do to me
I guess
This is payback
For the times
I didn't listen
You screamed and shouted and cried
But I said…nothing
I guess your showing me
What it feels
Like
To be on the
Other side of the silencer

**Deadweight written by Romeo and Wazo
(Jamey and Telemanchus)**

Love empowers me
I grit my teeth and strain
To maintain my equilibrium
And balance thru the pain
In my heart I know it's my duty
So with no hesitation I answer the call
Even though it's wearing me away
Preventing me from being my all
Every step is a little bit harder
Each stroke seems to bring me down
It's come to the point
That if I don't let you go then I too will drown
But I can't, I mustn't, I shouldn't give up
I'm loyal to the core
And my loyalties lie within my love
So I wouldn't want you to think I'm not loyal anymore
Though it hurts me deeply
I only have a little energy left
And in order to make it to the top
I can only carry myself
Hopefully someone stronger will come along
Still I wish you would've let me help you grow
Cause now I can no longer hold on to you
Sorry, but I must let you go

Decision, Decisions written by Jamey L. Wilkins

Stand or sit, speak or be silent
When my wellbeing is threatened
Should I declare peace or be violent
Stay or leave, argue or concede
My dignity is at stake
Do I beg or plead?
Fight or run, teach or be taught
Stock market shaky
Will I buy or be bought
Hide or seek, take heed or ignore
Limited supply
Accept less or get more
Be a predator or prey, give or try
Each decision may determine
If I live or die

Gangsta Booh written by Jamey L. Wilkins

Walk nasty
Talk jazzy
Neck twister
Finger snapper
Ass kicher
Damn I got a bad sister
Laugh with her
Cry wit her
Say the word
Rid with her
Street smart
Book smart
Angel face
Crook heart
Gangsta
The only word
That encompasses
Her confidence
Her trueness
Her coolness so foolish
Real sweet
Sourpuss
Mean mug
Jeans hug
Front like
She don't need love
Haters see
A tough bitch
Come wit
That rough shit

Leave with
A bust lip
Fly girl
My girl
My boo
I do
Eye you
Til I get an eyeful
But why do
You start shit
Always
Get smart wit me fo' I know… cause you gangsta

"Haitian Inspiration" written by Jamey L. Wilkins

I hear the crying from every nation
The sighing the trepidation (fear) (unease)
Tell me why you decided to violently wreck the Haitians
Went higher than expectations, the signs are in revelations
Hundred fifty thousand taken by scientist's estimations
While climbing through devastations
They're finding in excavations
Either bodies or children with all kinds of Deformations
Then nothing left them shaken
Lying on network stations
Calling it looting when truly survival was in abeyance
They're vying for extra rations
Tryna get explanations
Tryna find a reason why they're dying from desperation
For everything that taken
But why do you test our patience
Looking back I think you were just tired of segregation
Brought us together with no dividing or separation
From the lowest of the low to the highest of elevations
Doctors try and help the patients

Provide 'em with medication
Soothing the little babies that's crying their chests are aching
All the dust and all the smoke is denying them respiration
Still we acted with the swiftness of timing no hesitation
We found it's our second nature
When eyeing the desolation
That we're all the same creation it's time to suppress the hatred
And let love caress their faces
Survival and preservation
Those that's still alive are admired they're so courageous
Their mind is just amazing
'Stead of crying and forsaking
Let's find us some decoration
It's time for a celebration

Slavery written by Comrade Wazo (Jamey. Wilkins)

A slave is a slave is a slave. No matter, how fancy you dress him up, no matter how articulate or educated he may be; a slave is still a slave. It's a bit deeper than just the "slave mentality" rhetoric that some feel by acknowledging its existence means they are not a victim of it. The word slave brings to mind uneducated men transformed into beasts of burden. It brings to mind lynching, torture, rape, racism at its pinnacle. Slavery brings to mind whips and chains, plantations, cotton and of course "Massa." Just the word slave itself makes you think of a torn clothed, dirty barefoot blackman; it makes you think of Kunta…Kunta Kinte. It makes you think of everything you could not possibly be; it also makes you feel as though it could never happen to you. Like if you were alive back then you would've fought tooth and nail for your God-given right. Well the reality is you would not have, you would've woke yo' black Ass up, picked cotton, shined Massa's boot with your spit and then danced a jig if he told ya to. You would've broke a sweat hoping you'd find favor enough in his eyes to work in the house or to at least get first dibs on the leftovers, the scraps that they discarded as unworthy of being eaten. You know how I know, because you do it now. You are not built from the same fabric as Nat Turner, hell you aren't even on the same wavelength as

Harriet Tubman. She had more nuts than you'll ever have. Black Man.

You sit back and watch as police officers come to your city, your hood, your house and beat your brothers, cousins, son and fathers senseless. Why? because you are a slave. You get locked up due to a direct correlation to your environment and it's lack of necessities but abundance of drugs and weaponry and then even though in the streets you couldn't get a job worth working, you are forced to work for 40 cent a day in order to get gain time or just because they want you to work per the 13th amendment for it you do not you will spend your time in solitary confinement. Why! because you are a slave. You work on an average twice as hard in the lowest departments for not even half as much then are the first to call your supervisor (Massa) when a fellow worker or customer takes some of the product he helped make, produce, grow or package for himself hoping he'll promote you to a higher position (or the house) or give you something extra. Why? Because you are a slave. "Oh no, not me' you say, "I have graduated college. I'm an entrepreneur; I own my own business. I definitely am not a slave!" Okay smarty-pants, who gave you your education and taught you what they wanted you to know? Who allowed you to get your college grant/loan? Who allowed you to incorporate your business? Who do you pay rent to too set up shop on their land? Think about it. Think about all the people who did/do the exact same things you have and did not reach the same results. You are a minority; the majority does not succeed. Now ask yourself what is it about you that made you successful. What did they see in you that made them decide to allow you to advance? Please don't fool yourself by thinking you are smarter, worked harder or are special. Nah, I'll tell you what they saw in you, they saw a special kind of slave. You see you are just a developed slave, what back in the days they would've called an overseer. You are the slave that does not need physical chains because they taught you to be so smart that you are too stupid to run. They know yo'll prevent another brother from escaping even put your own life at risk to keep them straight. All while Massa sits back and get fat from the sweat of your brow. It is exactly this system that makes you a slave. The trick is simple but effective. One man with one gun with one bullet can lay down fifty people. All he has to do is pull it and shoot one person to emphasize who has the power. The rest will not move out of fear of being the next person shot. Now turn that negative scenario inside out to its positive counterpart (know and understand that Massa knows they both can have the same result) one group of people can keep a much larger group of people in check or let me say docile by allowing one to succeed. They only have one opening to fill but just the sight of that one person making it will give hope to the Massses making them feel that if they try hard enough or if they just do the right thing then they can also make it when in all actuality as in the first scenario they was only one.

To keep everyone filled with hope, every blue-moon they'll search for another potential developed slave who they already know will be so happy to have been chosen he'll only be an extension of them because this Sambo will bojangle, snitch or whatever it takes to stay in their good graces. Then in time he will forget that he was one of the subdued crowds, he will look down on them, criticize, berate and hate them for not achieving what he achieved. He will take on the traits of the Massa and hold them all at gunpoint for him. The crowd will then look at him as an Uncle Tom as house nigger, when ninety- nine percent of them would be him if given the chance. They'd love to be the unshackled slave not realizing in both cases they are still a slave a slave is a slave is a slave. I know some of you reading this may think I'm talking about you well I will save you the time I am! I want you to know I am talking about you, you ignorant, brown nosing…coward. You are not wiser nor did you make better decisions. The lesser of two evils is not a decision. To choose to not commit a crime but starve is not upstanding, righteous. Nor good. It's being stupid. To accept less than what you are supposed to have is not a wise move it's capitulation. Look at the maze surrounding you, it seems like each turn is a dead end and if not it's filled with trials and tribulations but one of them allows you to live. Nah, there are more than one that offer survival but what kind of survival? If you have to give up one freedom to get another, that's not life, that's slavery!

How about you stop going through the maze and go through the maze., Just bust this whole system to pieces and stake your claim. That's freedom. Anything less is slavery. It irks me when someone has the temerity to come out their mouth to say "Well you shouldn't have got locked up." This prison" like what the... spose to mean? They don't see that I am.... their cousin, brother, nephew, uncle, father, husband or son. They don't commend me for having the heart to fight back. They don't see that I am what they celebrate now but called stupid in the past. All of their civil rights leaders that they venerated today because they gave them the modicum of air that they call freedom were criminals, lawbreakers. But when I do it, when I resist, when I stand firm I am a fool. Well, I'd rather be a fool than a wise slave any day. Maybe one day they will understand. Maybe one day they will venerate me but I doubt you will. You know why? Cause you're a slave.

They came in Peace   J L. Wilkins

They came in peace
We left in chains
When they gave us freedom
We kept their names
How or why
Do we expect to change
Without understanding
The effects of shame
Accept the blame
For our next of kin
They came in peace
But we let them in
Allowed them in
Allowed them to sow
Their seeds of deceit
Without considering
It could lead to defeat
But they came in peace
How could we not greet them?
That exact train of thought
Helped them conquer our kingdoms
Obliterate our identity
Steal our legacy
Erase our history
Comprise our integrity
Destroy our religions
Everything we believed in
Then told us we were animals
Savages, heathens
They say they came in peace

With intentions to help
Like we were not able
To fend for ourselves
In actuality we were past
The primitive stage
The first civilization
While they were still living in caves
Nowadays our memory strayed
It's been corroded
The only thing we seem to know
Is what they told us?
We either rap
That way we'll never know
Who we truly are
They come in peace
But now they're called police
Aint nothing changed
Course we still leaving in chains
That's why they come in peace
In war they'd never take us
As one it couldn't be done
So they had to separate us
Now I don't know you
Neither do you know me
You use to be Kunta
But now you just Toby
My name is Jamey, had a daughter
And with pride I gave it to her
Never thought to ask my momma
Who gave it to her?
They came in peace
Told us to cover shame with pride

Used the truth
To fill our brain with lies
They came in peace
Now they're called the police
They think they're smart
And all of us beast
Changed from plantations
When slavery ended
To incarceration
And the 13th amendment
Exceptions exceptions
They came in peace
Deceptions, deceptions
And we think we free
Ha!

If you don't stand for something, you will fall for anything"
Written by Jamey L. Wilkins

How can this be? It is impossible to fall when you are not standing!!! But those that stand for something can fall for that very same thing; which in turn is their weakness, their Achilles heel. Once you know where a person stands you know where to attack them. By knowing where to attack them you can determine their strengths and weakness. You can diligently search for and find the chink in their armor. Once found you can predict their actions and once you can predict a person's reactions they can be manipulated. You are now able to use what they stand for to make them fall. If you have nothing to stand for, you have no discernable way of being attacked, because it will not be known what affects you and what doesn't. You will not know if you are feeding me or starving me. And I will not show outwardly any reaction for you to judge. Stoicism, look at water, it has no shape or form. Water can fit in anywhere and assume the shape of that space. Now look at ice, or frozen water, water that has chosen to take a stand. Ice cannot conform to another shape; it does not have the ability to change without breaking, or falling, or humbling itself and returning to water. Despair only affects those that have once achieved happiness a "fall from glory or grace." I you have nothing to counter paradise with, or nothing to contrast hell with, neither would exist or better yet both would exist as one, all in the same. Does it matter if it is hot or cold, if I could feel neither? It is said, "the bigger you are the harder you fall." The taller the building the longer it takes to hit the ground, thereby causing more damage. Once you commit yourself to something you invariably create unknown enemies. You have chosen a side to fight for and the fight is a never-ending fight you are the loser, which means either death or an end to your commitment. The way I see it, why fight period? That way you could not suffer defeat. The only thing to stand for is yourself…

Let me stop, sometimes I just let the pen walk across the page and let it lead me to where it wants to go. I love to take sayings or topics and express my view of them. I take my writing serious and I don't let people hear me unless I have perfected it. People in prison actually pay me to rap or write for them! I tend to "fall" back though because people tend to claim my words as theirs when I'm not around. Biting. I want to teach so bad what I know but understand a teacher's burden is much heavier than others and I am not built for it because I am not a practicer of what I preach at times. I'd rather put it on paper and let the reader get what he can out of it. But when I rap I've grown into more than a rapper I entertain crowds of people I've never received less than a perfect score in contests even when I went first! Speaking and rapping and writing are three totally different way of getting your point across though. When you perfect your gift; your stand will become more believable.

My parents taught me hate by JJB

For years I was penetrated too my bone,
I was taught hate
My parents told me this, there's a reason people
are dark, and people are light
The light represents beauty,
The dark represents ugly
I just listened patiently, being young, you don't
know wrong from right
What about their hair I asked my mother one
day?
Oh, she said, just look at their kinky hair
Yours baby girl, it long and bone strait.
But deep in my mind, it didn't seem right
Little children can't discern (distinguish) what is
wrong or right
Even though for years, I lived with the epitome
of hate
When I got older, the hate dissolved in my soul,
in its place was a chain of
pure love
Something I can't explain, it was if God's hands
had touched my soul
Grown now, with my own free will
I learn what this thing called hate can do and the
causalities it takes
Anything that arrives from hate, it's not good
It will hit home one day, give it some time and sit
back and wait
All my young life, hate corrupted my thoughts

It woke me up in the morning for breakfast and kissed me
Good-bye at night
Now, both my parents are in homes surrounded by caregivers, they
Taught me to hate
Now the cycle continues with the caregivers paying them back with more hate
I broke this abusive cycle; Giving thanks to God above
What arrives from God, it all about Love
Hate breeds pity and we don't need that
When Jesus died for us,
Folks it was all about love not HATE

Blood to blood, injustice Takes our own by JJB

Blood to blood, we are kin
Labor of pain that coats our sins
A dollar bill is less than a penny
A loaf of bread, few is fed
Blood to blood, no signs of
Change,
The fluorescent light
That hides the guilt of shame
Innocence lost, another youth is gone
With only skittles and a drink
In the summer rain
"On the shoulder of giants" we must revisit our
thoughts
Step by step and revisit their walks
We can't let this death defeat our efforts even
though
Our life may ever be affected
To the gesture of a mother's kiss
To mourning of our fallen son
No power lies in hate
"Splendor in the grass" rests in the memory
On this young child's face
Tick tock, time passes, a frown face
A clown laughs
Blood to blood,
Unblemished to the signs of pain
God gives us life, but man takes it in vain

Skit: Dave are You Ready? By JJB

If a lady is performing this Skit and is the main character, her name would be Sadie
Characters: Dave, Death and Greed
Plot: Dave is in his early twenties; he is a drug dealer and a gangbanger.
His life is filled with corruption and violence.
His motto "kill or make a deal"
Everyone has a price, he thought.
Little does Dave know, Death awaits him anytime now
Narrator: The time is 2:15 p.m.
Dave is making one of his many drug runs at the *City Lake*. Nothing is unusual, but today he's having a funny feeling about this run. Dave gets ready to make his drop. He drives his Mercedes up to his favorite spot, the City Lake. After the drop, he starts his daily run.
He runs at least two miles a day but as he is running this particular day, he notices a stranger watching him carefully.
Being a drug dealer, he was always observant of his surroundings.
Narrator: The last round, Dave could see out of the corner of his eyes that the stranger was running towards him and in his hand was a 22-caliber pistol. Instantly, he started running to his car because he wasn't strapped. But before he could reach his car, bullets were flying all over the place and one hit him in the left arm.
Storyline Starts:

Death: Wake up my son!
Narrator: Dave woke up in the hospital with his arm in a sling
Strange man sitting on his bed.
Dave: arrrrrrrrrr, what happen? Am I dead?
Death: No! But you were only an hourglass away because
 When life is no more, Ha, Ha, my time has come.
Dave: then excuse me, who are you? And why are you here? (Looking sarcastic)
Death: You, my son was given a second chance but before my cloak could knock on the door, God extended out his hand and gave you another chance. But due to your life choices, I'll be back!
Dave: It wasn't a dream. Scratching his head, I was lucky this time
But I'm a gangster, no bullets will slow my roll
I will play harder, live larger and recruit more fools to kill,
If they don't have my dollar bills.
And if you think I'm playing, just ask the victim up the street.
 I hit hard and slow, preying on the weak.
Bang Bang kill or be killed, this is my reality
And baby, it's my time, and I'm for real.
Narrator: 5 years later, no change in Dave's behavior.
Narrator: Dave had started slippin! Making drug runs alone, not taking his bodyguards, this guy thought he was untouchable
Death: Knock, knock
Dave: the door opens

Death: walks in
Dave: You look like this cat called Death, but you couldn't be
I'm in my twenties, it's not my time.
Death: Ha, Ha, my son, this is he
Action: pointing his fingers at Dave while ice shoots forward
Death: but I'm on a mission, try some of that power
in your pocket, it won't hurt you; you are the man! You can handle it!
Dave: I'm a gang banger and dope pusher, look at my new red shoes!
Death: Action (Getting bad) Try it; try it!
Narrator: After years of seeing drug addicts sniff and shoot up, Dave wanted to taste the chase and he was in a haste
Death: That's right, try it! Try it!
Dave: Okay" (getting mad.)
Narrator: Dave gets his syringe, his needle and his spoon.
Dave mixed the heroin and asked his buddy to shoot him up before noon.
Death: Com on speed it up
Bill down the street I got to make another run and give him the same treat
Dave: Oh, I'm flying! There's no pain, this stuff is great!
Narrator: Then Dave realized; he had just shot up the pure stuff
Dave thought about his grandmother. The beautiful lady and how she was vain to the end.

(Narrator signals for the Beautiful Lady skit to begin while life is flashing before Dave's eyes) Song: *Crazy in Love with you by Queen B.*
Narrator: signals to resume skit Dave Are You Ready>>>>>>>
Death: Ha! Ha you fool, I told you I'll be back one day and 'today is your day!"
Narrator: Dave looked at his friend Greed, but was he really a friend?
Greed: Don't read, (this is action!) Take the mask off his face, all his sins are exposed.
Stickers with money on his face, fame and materialistic.
Death: Greed, thank you for your help!
Narrator: They gave each other a high five!

Greed: Money and Fame, helps Ole Greed be on his a game.
I roll hard and slow, disguising myself as someone's friend
And when it's all said and done their dignity is gone and just like a bird, Ole Greed fly on to another home
Ha, Ha, I'm greed,
Death: Gives Greed a high-five, don't get mad, you have a choice. One day Ole death will be wiped away, but until that day "my rage will continue to run rampant like wild fires smothering victims while they sleep. Let me give you a tip by chance if you want to speed up your time, ha, ha, ole death don't even mind. Even for the pure at

heart when they fall asleep, they have hope. But, let Ole death tell you this, this hope doesn't apply to evildoers. It depends on you, you have two choices, so what you gonna do? I'm waiting! **Because Ole death *doesn't take off for any occasions.***

"Death and the Beautiful Lady"

Script: Death and the Beautiful Lady by JJB
Plot: The beautiful lady based her life on her outward appearance, she was vain, insolent (rude) but she was beautiful and that's all she needed.
Narrator: The beautiful lady lived her life doing what she please, why because she could. Vain was her DNA and Beauty crippled her to fame. But, little did the Beautiful lady know, death would be scheduling his visit soon. Time isn't promised to us, when I think back, I think about my friend, the beautiful lady. The beautiful lady's beauty was known from coast to coast, she was very exquisite in appearance causing men to fall at her feet and beg to breathe the air next to her and boy she was very vain. Every time I think of my friend, the beautiful lady, I cry, I just cry!
Song: "Crazy in Love with You"
Beautiful Lady: Dancing as she gazes into the mirror and talking: Yes, I'm vain, yes, I know I'm beautiful!
How many women can match my beauty? I can get whomever I please!
Ha Ha!
B. lady: Strutting back and forth admiring herself while dancing to "Crazy in Love with You"
Death: knocks on the beautiful lady's door
 The beautiful lady:

Come
On
In!
Death: beautiful lady, I see you still admiring yourself, and rightfully so, my god you are beautiful

The beautiful lady: Looking the man up and down
Who, who, who are you? How do you know my name? I never seen you in my circle of friends!

Narrator: Death was dressed in black with pearly white teeth, and whatever planet this cat came from, it had to be saturated with dough. But he had something that most of the men the beautiful lady knew didn't have, he was just as breathtaking

beautiful as she. But what was on his fingers, it looked like rings made out of icicles.

The beautiful lady: Looking confuse, she dismissed her doubts as him being cool. Eyeing him up and down, this one, she thought could be added to her collection.

The beautiful lady: I didn't catch your name

Death:
just slipped in a spell, my name is Deathhhhhhhhhhhhhhhh

The Beautiful lady: What kind of name is that?

Death: It's a name not of my choosing but it excites fear, Ha, ha

The beautiful lady: Noticed cool air coming from his mouth

Acting out (Now, she was afraid!) What, I'm young. Look at me! I'm too beautiful to cross that bridge.

Death: aw, you are beautiful so beautiful that make ole death want to go the other way

Action: sucking his teeth while he struts back and forth

But one day, one day, I will be back! But you don't have to worry today, I was just sliding by because ole Slow Walk up the street, is on his last round with his bottle of special wine.

Ha, ha

The beautiful lady: saying out loud. This is crazy, there is no such man called death

Narrator: The beautiful lady: went wild, she lived her life harder, dated more men, and created more confusion with the lovers she done wrong.

Narrator: The years had not been kind to the beautiful lady; she had several heart attaches and health issues had finally slowed her down. And her friends, well, they were nonexistence. Her ex-friends weren't true friends, they were vain also; they didn't have time for a person slowed down with illnesses. The beautiful lady hours in the mirror was nonexistence. Most of her time was spent in and out of the doctors' offices.

Death: Knock, Knock

The beautiful lady: Come Come, Oh, I remember you, you're my friend (Death), with your bad self!

You haven't age a bit.

The Beautiful Lady: still tryin to bust a move,

Death: shaking his head
Death: yes, beautiful lady, this is he
Beautiful lady: What Going on death? Are you going back to Slow Walk's House?
Death: No Beautiful lady, this stop is for youuuuuuuuuuuuuuuuuuuuuuuuuu!
The beautiful lady: Backing up, no, no, it's not me, I'm still healthy
Death: Really, beautiful lady, you had several heart attacks. Your legs are shot, most of your time is spent in an out of hospitals.
Beautiful lady: but I thought, I would have more time.
Death: Beautiful lady, look at you! You came limping to the door. You don't live your life in the mirror anymore, why? (Throwing up his hands)

Beautiful lady: Well, the person staring back in the mirror, isn't me, it's a strange looking old woman
Narrator/Death: beautiful lady why can't you face realty, you are the little old person staring back in the mirror, you still are beautiful, little has changed but where the dimples were, now, there're wrinkles. All your life you worshipped what was in the mirror. All your life, you used your beauty in the worse way. Basing your life on an unreal façade. Leaving causalities along the road of despair.
The beautiful lady: drops on her knees and became praying and crying
Death: touching beautiful lady, child, please, let it go because ole "death creeps like a thief in the

night" and whether you prepare or not, the time is right.

Beautiful Lady: you ain't no man, if you were a man you would be powerless against my beauty! (Falling) Narrator: the beautiful lady's life began to flash before her eyes (dancing), partying and Loving: **Song: "*Slim and the Supreme Angels*," Death and the Beautiful lady**

In Memory of my friend, Linda T.

That Child by JJB

That child
Caused a nation to uncover its hate
That child
Caused profiling to be a sign to kill a child
And left him lying in the dirt
That child
Caused people to look at the disparities
In the court system
Making stricter Laws for blacks
While some whites get a pat on their back
That child
Allowed us to mourn and look for answers
From God
That child
Allowed us to uncover the hidden
Agenda that racist strive as a sore
Running wild
That child
Caused a nation to be divided through racial lines
That child
Cause me to shed tears for my sons
While others sought protection from God
But all and all
That child made a nation realized that we are
Not yet free
Free just to be

The Talk by JJB

I was motivated to write this piece because in a Nation of plenty, racism still exists. Blacks are still profiled and treated inhumanly. Just maybe one day, we will be free, free to be.

Boy: Momma I was stopped by the police
Momma: Lord, no, no
Boy: Momma they called me out of my name,
Hand-cupped me while they
Laughed in the street
Momma: No, no
Boy: Momma after they disregarded my rights,
They told me to take my ragged tail home
Momma: NOOOOOOOOOOOOOOO
Boy: Momma why didn't you give me the talk
Momma: Child do ya remember when I came in your room late one night,
And told ya the hours had come
Boy: Yes momma
Momma: I knew the fall had arrived
Boy: what do you mean momma
Momma: Son, you are a black man in a white man's world
It time for you
To watch every step you take and humble yourself if you
Are stopped by the police and searched
Boy; But momma I thought you were half sleep to say the
Fall was about to come, it made no sense

Momma: I said that to prepare you my child for this
Boy: What is the fall momma?
Momma: all your life my child you will
Be measured by a stick,
Boy: a stick
Momma: you were stopped my son for no probable cause,
Boy: Wha what
Momma: Son, da da days have come;
Roll your sleeve up higher and
Release your pride in the sky
Boy: Oh, I think I understand momma,
It takes a man to be humble
Because when they were calling me names,
I smiled and said I'm a man
They call me V.I.P
Momma: That's right my child
Boy: I was polite momma; I was calm and I kept my cool
I had my phone in my pocket ready to dial
a number in case of the fall
Then I remember what you said
If we walk without God, we don't stand a chance
Momma: I see, I see, my son
There will come a day when all black boys
Must hear the talk
Boy: Momma, muddy waters drenched my eyes
Sweet defeat enticed my cheeks
But momma, I didn't bow my head in shame
Or stumble and say, "Boy is not my name."

I smiled and said "my momma taught me my name at the ripe age of one
She taught me pride every day before I stepped out the front door."
She said, "Child never bow your head in shame"
It's an honor because God never play games
So when I was stopped by the cops
Pride welcomed me as a friend
And pride kept me strong, proud to be a young black man

Questions yourself

Do you know anybody that has experienced mental and physical abuse?
Do you know anyone that was molested?
Do you know anyone that seek out men/women for their own gratification?
Do you know anyone beaten down by this system?
Do you know anyone that has totally given up?

Child Speak Out was a healing process for me, it allowed me to pour out my innermost thoughts and release the built-up anger that was hidden behind my closely kept façade.

It is my hope that this would allow you to open up and find comfort in knowing that you can release your pain in a positive way to help others in your quest to find a better space.

Bullying hurts by JJB

I watched my best friend become the target practice of bullying

What did I do? Absolutely nothing! Now, my friend is gone

Bullying in any form is wrong, sure you say it's a harmless joke, a childish prank

"You need to have tougher skin," they said

But I witnessed firsthand the bleeding tears, the one-sided looks, signaling me to step in

Meanwhile, I laughed a nervous laugh

Overlooking the knots churning around in my throat

While my friend stared back at me with blank stares

Regrets are sometimes the signs of a wanna be hero

But in reality, I'm just like most of you, you know who I'm talking about

But I have no time to place blames, my work has just begun, roaring like a lion, I will lend my voice to the one who can't fight these roads alone

I will pucker up strength within myself and dare anyone who tries to bully someone in my presence. Pacing and timing for these cowards are all I need, then I will leap forward and defend the voiceless. I roar and Roar. I come not to be a follower of the cause but to lift my friends up before they fall, what gives me strength, I remember my friend, the one people called a coward!

Yes, I envision his smile as he told me about all his aspirations. To me he wasn't a coward, *he was my little brother.*

Forbidden Fruit by Jamey Wilkins (Skit, two person)

It's not that you're more attractive

Yet I'm more attracted to you

Inexplicably drawn as if you were magnetized

I know I shouldn't but I have to try

Passersby

Cut their eye, turn up their noses

But I don't notice

Or should I say I don't pay attention

Because I'm focused

On you

So tempting, so strange, so taboo

A forbidden fruit

That I selfishly bit into

I'm used to dealing with women who

Are supposedly meant for me

But for some reason I see things differently

I see you I see them, but they are see through

They are not equal

But does that mean you are more than?

With you I am the richest poor man

With them I am the brokest rich man

I should be proud, I know this is a blessing

Still I'm cursed by our connection

Your essence is deceptive

Far from my reflection

Yet there you are staring back at me

The perfect contrast to me

Heading for a catastrophe

I know that you are bad for me

History speaks to me, scolds me with vivid imagery

Of our troublesome past that outlasts my memory

Remember we, snuck out just to be together

You said to please me, you would be whatever

And you would do whatever

And for some reason it felt better

I don't know why, I can't explain it

A definition for this I don't have

Even though this won't last, shouldn't last

It couldn't last

It's lasting long enough

I've been fasting long enough

So I sate my distinguished taste

Until I'm full and might hurl

I'm black and I'm proud so stay away from me white girl?

Never Got (Love at First Sight) by Jamey Lamont Wilkins

I would say you soft but I never got to touch you

Never got to taste you so I can't say you sweet

Figure I would spoil you if I ever got to love you

But I never got the chance cause we never got to speak

Never got to sleep so I won't say you're my dream girl

Won't know how you feel cause we never got to kick it

Never looked up love so I don't know what it means girl

The reason I ain't call cause I never got ya digits

Somehow it seems funny, tho' you never got the joke

That I never got to tell ya so you never got to laugh at

Went and bought a stamp put it on my envelope

But you never got the letter cause I never got yo' address

I would never cheat on you lie to you or beat you

When I looked into your eyes my mouth never got the words

Promised myself I would say it if I ever got to meet you

But I never did it cause I never got the nerve

Baby if it's meant to be then one day it'll happen

Destiny is something that you never got to plan

Never got ya' attention I was slipping when you passed met

Now I'll never know cause you already got a man

Must Keep on By JJB

Must keep on

I cannot lose

To slay the dragon

And to empower my children

I must make a

Shield of armor that will not break

Must keep on

I can't lose this fight

The dragon waits in hiding

Whether he is a predator or prey, I can't say

I might be exhausted

I might be fatigued

But to slaughter this dragon

I must stay alert

"But woe to the earth" because the

Dragon has come out of hiding

And boy he is ready to fight

Please ask yourself this,

Are you asleep or are you awake?

Keep your shield close to your heart

And with God's help

You will win this fight

> *"When you try to block other people blessings*
> *You will not receive your own"*

Lovers of the Flesh by Josephine Jenkins Bridgers

Lovers of the utmost qualities
Passion drove me to overlook whatever
Boundaries there were, yes!
Desires of the flesh conquered all my doubts
Was I a lover in the moment, awe! With raging desires, let me think.
Finally, I was caressed, after years of absentee and empty beds.
Now my flesh is warm from the body of my lover
Will this passion last forever?
Who knows?
But for today, my cup is filled from the thirst of his kisses.

Remembering my sister, Dorothy Jenkins

I used this as a platform to speak for my sister since she can't speak for herself. Dorothy died from Breast Cancer, but before she died, she was abused by a system that she had supported for years.

Dorothy was fired after working years for Nash County Correction System, because she wouldn't lie and say an inmate confessed to her. She was interrogated like a criminal and when she didn't say what they wanted her to say, the abusers told her they would make sure she lose her job.

The reason this is relevant, is because if this happened to Dorothy, a law-abiding citizen, this misconduct could happen to you.

There are some good, and decent officers that represent the law, but the ones that will do anything to get a conviction need to be weeded out because they truly are a danger to our democracy.

My sister attempted to seek justice before she died by naming the officers involved with legal representation, but her lawyer made an error and her case was dismissed.

Dorothy's health deteriorated, and she died very heartbroken; a person fighting for their life doesn't need this, that is why God gave me the platform to speak for her and let the people who were involved know that Dorothy's voice will be heard.

But, if my sister had won her case before she died, her husband would have reaped the benefits. This man didn't deserve a dime; let alone a settlement.

I was brokenhearted about the dismissal of my sister's case because I felt her pain. She struggled to breathe and could barely walked while she sought to fight for her rights knowing that it was a taste because dying was knocking at her door.

The last days of her life, she let her husband come back but regretted her reasoning process for being so naïve. If Dot's lawyer had did his job, she would have won her case and monetary compensation would have followed

After years of asking myself why, a Bible verse comes to mind, "you gonna reap what you sow" How can you hate your neighbor and love God? That's why this platform is the perfect one to let people know that sometimes their gifts can come to them as a friend.

Whatever platform you have, use it wisely!

For those of you out there who think, this could never happen to you, this world has changed. Let us keep on striving to make this world a better place with the truth.

Think Positive by Lillian Jenkins

When there is a thunderstorm that darkens the beautiful sky, you know the radiant sun will shine again. When there is a winter blizzard that chills you down to your bones, you know mother earth will cover you with a warm blanket once again and when sadness grips you by the hand and will not let you go, you know happiness will guide you away with a sudden mercifulness in perfect timing, so let us think positive no matter what befalls us, because one day, all our positive thoughts may bring Joy, may bring happiness, may bring peace and may all our hopes and dreams come true!

Feelings by Erica Davis

The doors are locked, and the key is within your soul. Your happiness is light, your anger is bold. Your tears hurt with pain from the heart. Your mind is dark with fears deep inside the heart. You clutch your chest with the feeling of love. The loss of passionate, affection from your soul. You dreamed of waking up one day, living in a fairy tale but you and I both know that this world is more like a living nightmare. The loving world, that you once saw, is almost unrecognizable. Your eyes tend to swell up with thoughts of despair. Your words seem to make no sense when it comes to walking in thin air. The lightning that surrounds the stormy sky is filled with rage. The emotional outrage takes the stage. Happiness is there in the light. Darkness scares it away with fresh delight. But do not be afraid by these harmful emotions, for they should not scare you. Who are you to say I cannot! Who are you to say happiness is no longer my friend. You can see straight through the light. A person's mind can be their private enemy. Do not be afraid to let yourself speak for light is in the air. You shall speak! You unlocked the door which was once locked. You unclench your chest which was once held like a pouch. You stop sobbing and crying, for now you can **speak! Happiness is in your soul for you to keep!**

Guard your heart by Lillian Jenkins

"How do you mend a broken heart" is a question many have asked?
And up to this point it has been a dawning task
because feelings are involved
Which makes this question hard to solve
However, the answer to this question comes from within
Time is the healer, but negative thinking is the
Killer
You see, your heart is not really broken, your
Mind uses this excuse as a token
In the mind you control all vital organs
The heart is the most precious, so it should be
Guarded, so cherish it my friend, and it may ache but with a strong mind, you will be determined not
To let it break

War by Erica Davis

In the dark days of a person's mind, I ask, do all they think of is hate, for man shall do what they want by thee. We have no control. The lack of love for each other is always gonna to cause war. From the East to the South, we no longer hear children singing. From the North to the West, we no longer hear school bells ringing. From nation to nation, we lose our trust…From people to people, we return to dust. From the unborn child in the mother's womb that depends on her breathing to stay alive…
My dear brother, I call to you, will you help m! I am wounded. You may hear, but my dear brother is cruel to the soul. The world may care some, but this world is not yet free…free from disasters that fight in the evening. From country to country, the world burns down. From mind to mind, they began to frown. Smile to smile they decrease. Laughter to laughter, they decease. Breath to breath, they stop breathing. Heart to heart, they stop beating! Human to human, who do we trust? War! We all return to dust

Black on black crime

We should be just as passionate about this, as we are when we hear about a shooting of an unarmed black by a white person. If you look at it logically, a crime is a crime.
But what make it different, is the cover ups, and no accountabilities for the murderers' actions.
Every time you find these murderers not guilty, that mean they are sent back
into our communities putting more potential victims at risk.
Ask yourself why!
When officers break the law, let the law be a model that is applied to their misconducts instead of justifying the unthinkable, causing people to seek justice in the streets. Why are the shield of silence centered around these murderers? They are not worthy of being called officers of the law; we all should be embarrassed.
Also, black on black crime, it's sad and very disturbing. We fought and died for freedom, now you shot your brother/sister for no justification: shoes, drugs, disputes, etc.
We fought for, the right to live and strive. Take a history lesson to improve your critical thinking, because all lives matter.
Think! Don't let someone else seal your fate.

Miracles Do Happen

For those out there who don't believe, Miracles do happen.

Della is a testimony because when the doctor told us it was nothing in his power to do for her feet and they needed to be cut off; my sister said "No!" Della feet had gangrene and there were no hope saving her feet, but the power of prayer, restored her feet.

Della's feet had no blood supply because her legs had become inactivity due to two knee surgeries in which she wasn't active causing her knees to buckle up. But we prayed and prayed and then, we saw the power of God restoring blood supply to her feet, healing them.

When we went back to the doctor after he told us he needed to cut off her feet, he looked puzzled, then questioned us about what happen?

Next visit, same thing, he questioned us and told us to keep doing what we were doing.

Now, can you imagine living and seeing this miracle first-hand?

It restored our hope because God answered our prayers and Della is a living testimony.

www.ingramcontent.com/pod-product-compliance
Lightning Source LLC
Chambersburg PA
CBHW031409290426
44110CB00011B/314